Mastering the
Essay

Advanced Writing
& Historical Thinking Skills

AP* World History Edition

Instructional Handbook

by Tony Maccarella

REVISED EDITION

Includes the Summer 2017 Course Revisions

Sherpa Learning is dedicated to helping high-achieving learners gain access to high-quality, skills-based instruction that is created, reviewed, and tested by teachers. To learn more about Sherpa Learning and our vision, or to learn about some of our upcoming projects, please visit us at **www.sherpalearning.com**.

Publisher/Editor: David Nazarian

Copy-Editor/Permissions: Christine DeFranco

Cartographer: Sal Esposito

Cover Image: View of Mt Fuji from Chureito Pagoda,
© Ryusakimaou/Dreamstime.com

This edition has been revised to reflect changes that were made to the course and exam by the College Board® in the Summer of 2017.

* AP is a registered trademark of the College Board, which was not involved in the production of, and does not endorse, this product.

ISBN 978-0-9905471-6-7

SHERPALEARNING
GUIDING YOU TO EVEN GREATER HEIGHTS

Printed in the United States of America.

10 9 8 7 6 5 4 3

This book is dedicated to my dad, who taught me the value of seeing things through to the end. Without him, this book would be just another dream.

Wish you were here to see it, Dad.

Table of Contents

Table of Contents

Introduction

If you are like most AP World History students, you are concerned that you may not know enough facts to score well on the Multiple-Choice section of the exam, and you are probably not-just-a-little intimidated by the prospect of a brand new AP exam format that includes Short-Answer Questions and two thesis essays, one of which is the always-mysterious Document-Based Question (DBQ). You have, no doubt, heard that these essays are all hand-scored by unknown people in unknown places, each certain to apply his or her own standards of quality to the task. Since you have no way of controlling who scores your essays, or which standards they apply, you are relying on the Multiple-Choice Questions to carry your score. You're not about to take chances and just hope you and the mystery reader are on the same page. As a result, you are probably somewhat dismayed by the lack of review terms and multiple-choice practice questions in this book, and are wondering where you can buy a "real" AP prep book.

Fear not! *Mastering the Essay* is better than AP prep books because this book focuses on the often-neglected part of the exam—the part that *will* make or break your score—the essays. If the previous paragraph describes you, then the first thing you must learn is that most of your preconceptions about the essay section of the AP exam are absolutely false. The AP readers who score your essays are high school teachers and college professors—people not often known for their mysterious origins. Even less mysterious are the standards by which the essays are assessed. The College Board® (the organization that writes the AP exam) has created very clear guidelines for assessment, and the test-makers spend many hours training each reader to apply these standards accurately and consistently. In fact, your essay will almost certainly receive the same score regardless of which of the AP readers assess it.

I am one of those AP readers, and I have written this book to help you, the AP World History student, learn the standards by which your essays will be scored. By learning what's needed for a top score, you will be better prepared to incorporate these things into your essays. Even the very-scary DBQ is scored according to these standards. Developing the necessary skills to succeed on the AP essays will not be an overnight task, but if you follow the step-by-step process detailed in the pages that follow, before you know it, you will be writing essays that regularly score at the top end of the AP World History rubrics.

As an added bonus to using *Mastering the Essay* instead of some run-of-the-mill AP prep book, the skills needed for writing great AP World History essays are the exact skills needed for writing great college-level history essays. Rather than wasting months preparing for a single day in May, spending time developing better writing skills with *MTE* is an investment in college success. So put the prep books back on the shelf—*Mastering the Essay* is the only "prep" you need to achieve the highest score on the AP World History exam and to write college-level thesis essays.

I have designed each unit to explain one particular part of the writing process. To assist in developing your skills, each instructional section is accompanied by a set of practice exercises in the Exercise Workbook. I set out to make this book useful to students in any AP World History class, no matter which specific topic is being studied. Each exercise set is divided into chronological practice questions that mirror the new AP Course Outline provided by the College Board®. These general chronological divisions should permit you the greatest chance of practicing your skills within the context of the particular period of history being studied in your class.

So let's get started. Part 1 begins by demystifying the AP essay rubrics and outlining the writing process. In Part 2, we break down each step and provide dozens of practice exercises so you can master the process. Finally, we introduce the new Multiple-Choice Question format and tackle the new Short-Answer Question type. Read and practice the steps, read your textbook, take good notes in class, and by May, you will be prepared to achieve the highest score on the AP World History exam. Good luck and write on!

Tony Maccarella

How to Use this Book

Guided Practice

Mastering the Essay contains Guided Practice exercises to help you understand the six steps of the *MTE* writing process found in Part 2 of this book.

Each Guided Practice activity connects to a set of exercises in the Exercise Workbook.

Chronological Periods

Because most World History teachers deliver their courses chronologically, each set of exercises in the Workbook contains skills-based items organized into chronological eras. This organization will help you to apply the information you are learning in school to each of the writing-skills exercises.

Choices

New skills will be introduced in each chapter, while skills learned in earlier chapters are continually reinforced. You may choose to practice each step of the writing process using the exercises most appropriate to the historical content your class is covering at that moment. Or you may choose to complete all the exercises in the workbook and develop good writing habits, while reviewing *all* aspects of world history. The choice is yours.

Additional Resources

Visit the companion website for additional resources and valuable updates!

www.sherpalearning.com/mte

Part 1
Before You Begin

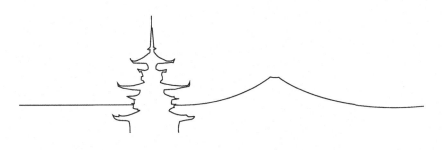

The Key to the AP Exam

A few years ago, in my first AP textbook, I argued that "the only skill that truly matters on an AP History exam is writing." Now, however, the AP World History exam has changed, so it's time to reevaluate. The redesigned exam has fewer Multiple-Choice Questions, a new Document-Based Question format, a single Free-Response Question (now called the Long Essay Question), and several Short-Answer Questions. So guess what? On the new exam, writing matters even more!

Most other books claiming to help improve your AP exam score are based on the assumption that success on the exam depends on your ability to recall historical facts. That is why so many of them devote hundreds of pages to reviewing historical content. Unfortunately, this assumption ignores several interesting statistics published by the College Board®, the organization that writes, administers, and scores the AP exam.

Did you know, for instance, that more than half of all students who scored a 4 or 5 on the old AP exam actually scored lower than 60% on the multiple-choice section[1] (the part of the test in which content seems to matter most)? This means that the majority of students whose scores qualify them for college credit get almost half of the Multiple-Choice Questions wrong. They did, however, achieve a top score on their essays. At the same time, many students who scored better than 50% on the multiple-choice section ended up getting a score of less than 4 on the exam, overall, if their essay scores were low.[2] **Bottom line—the key to a great score on the AP exam is good writing!**

I help score the essays for the AP European History exam. I know, from years of firsthand experience, what it takes to earn a top score on AP history essays, and I've written this book to share that

1, 2 – http://research.collegeboard.org/programs/ap/data

knowledge with students and teachers. The process outlined in this book is not a secret formula and the College Board® will not disqualify your score for using this process. In fact, the creators of the test want you to know how to write better essays. Better essays mean higher scores, and higher scores demonstrate to colleges and universities the value of an Advanced Placement education. Just as it is not a secret formula, this process is also not a magic potion. Just reading this book will not improve your score. Before you can see any real improvement in your score, you must practice—and master—the steps of the *MTE* writing process. That is precisely the reason why *MTE* includes 100+ exercises, including 30 full-length Document-Based Questions (DBQs).

Let's be clear about one thing before we move ahead: just because writing is the key to a great score, that doesn't let you off the hook when it comes to studying. **Read your textbook!** You must know your history in order to achieve the highest scores on your essays. Content is not the key to the exam, but it still matters.

Understanding the Process

Considering that I've written a book about how to write strong, high-scoring essays, you might think that my students spend hours each week writing essay after essay. Not so. In fact, many of my students become uneasy when, for the first several months of the school year, they've been asked to write few, if any, full-length essays. During those months, they practice developing strong thesis statements and outlines—but no essays. By winter recess, some of them are actually a bit anxious, fearing that they should have been writing more.

It's not until the second semester rolls around that I ask them to try their hands at a complete essay. When they do, they are pleasantly surprised with the results. This is because, by that time, they have learned the most important lesson for mastering the essay: in order to produce a quality essay, it is essential to perfect the thesis and outline first.

To understand my reasoning, take a look at the AP Long Essay Question rubric. Of the 6 possible points awarded for the LEQ:

1 point is available in Part A – Thesis

1 point is possible in Part B – Contextualization (essentially, framing your argument)

2 points can be earned in Part D – Analysis & Reasoning (the logic & complexity of your argument)

That's 4 out of 6 points for thesis and argument—all the result of careful prewriting, which is evident in the opening paragraph of your essay. The remaining 2 points are awarded for Evidence Analysis, and although that is certainly best accomplished within the body of the essay, effective evidence analysis results from combining evidence you've brainstormed from the outset with the argument you've developed in your opening.

Even though the new essay rubrics look very different from those used with the old exam, in fact, these new rubrics award points for exactly the same key characteristics that make any essay great— *thesis, organization,* and *evidence*. And just as in the past, two of those three can be established in the opening paragraph, before any specific evidence is introduced.

Readers of AP exam essays consistently point to the thesis as the key feature in determining the quality of an essay. A high-quality thesis does more than simply answer the question; it outlines the argument in terms of how you will present evidence and why that evidence matters. After reading a high-quality thesis, the AP reader will have a fairly reliable idea of where the essay will fall on the rubric, in terms of thesis and organization. This is why my students spend half the year writing only theses and outlines. By February, they are skilled at developing two of the three key characteristics assessed on the LEQ rubric. Since they have completed most of the course content by that time, they have all the necessary evidence to tackle the third characteristic with very little trouble.

Is it possible to begin with a weak thesis and improve the essay within the body paragraphs? Yes, but without a well-organized opening, it is much more difficult to develop your argument. Remember that AP readers are humans, and all humans are subject to their own predispositions. Appeal to those predispositions! Take the time to craft a solid thesis and use it to develop a well-organized and comprehensive essay that your readers will appreciate. Since many of the AP readers are university professors, it should be no surprise that success on your college essays will rely very heavily on the same key characteristics found in your AP essays.

Introduction to the AP Rubrics

Like many other writing rubrics, the AP rubrics are designed to standardize the scoring process. In other words, they make the essays "more fair." Their design allows hundreds of trained readers to assess each essay in exactly the same way. That means, no matter who reads your essay, you are likely to achieve the same score. As you might imagine, any rubric that yields this level of consistency is also quite predictable. If you are trained to use the AP rubrics, you can identify the characteristics of a strong essay; and if you can identify the things that make a strong essay, you will find it easier to include those things within your own work.

As mentioned above, the AP rubrics have been redesigned. The new rubrics look very different from those we have used for the past decade or so. As you might expect, teachers who have worked with AP for a while have spent the past couple of years critiquing these new rubrics. In fact, the College Board® has responded with several tweaks to improve the new rubrics. But don't worry! Good writing is still good writing, and a well-written thesis essay will still be rewarded on the AP World History exam.

While many have argued that all sorts of politics and bureaucratic haggling went into the new rubric structure established by the College Board®, above all the din sits one supreme truth—the AP exam must remain relevant to the demands of higher education if it is to survive. If you remember this one truth, you will have no trouble understanding why any AP essay rubric will ultimately reward the attributes most closely associated with excellent college essays. So relax about the changes and let's dive in and learn more about the rubrics.

As discussed earlier, there are two essay questions on the AP World History exam—the Long Essay Question (LEQ) and the Document-Based Question (DBQ). Unlike the old essays, responses to the new questions are scored neither holistically, nor on a core checklist. The new rubrics utilize a hybrid format, but the easiest way to understand them might be to forget about their format and just look closely at the descriptive text within each rubric category.

AP World History LEQ Rubric

The LEQ rubric is divided into the following four parts: **Thesis, Contextualization, Evidence,** and **Analysis & Reasoning**. Let's start with the most essential piece of any thesis essay—the thesis.

Thesis (1 point)

In order to earn the one point assigned in the Thesis section of the rubric, you must create a thesis statement that responds directly to all parts of the question, and you must place that statement within your opening or closing paragraph. That's it! Simply answer the question and write your answer in the first or last paragraph. But, don't forget that an excellent thesis might help you to earn an additional point or two in the fourth part of the rubric—Analysis & Reasoning.

Contextualization (1 point)

In addition to developing a logical argument that demonstrates a complete understanding of the specific question you've chosen to answer, the College Board® wants you to demonstrate an understanding of the historical context of your argument. If you open your essay with a few statements that describe the historical setting within which your argument is best understood, you will earn this point. We will address several of the best options for accomplishing this goal.

Evidence (2 points)

The Evidence section of the rubric is the part that rewards you for all those long hours spent memorizing details. If you mention a few specific examples with relevance to the question prompt, you can earn the first of the two points. If you connect that evidence to your thesis, you will get the second point, as well. *Mastering the Essay* devotes an entire unit to evidence and its use within your argument, so these points will be yours, too.

Analysis & Reasoning (2 points)

The College Board® wants students to demonstrate an ability to think like professional historians. To that end, the rubrics seek to reward specific historical argument techniques—*Comparison, Causation*, and *Change and Continuity Over Time* (CCOT). Depending on the essay prompt, you must create a response that takes the form of one of these specific argument-types.

Since your thesis tells the reader what you intend to say, and an analytical thesis describes how you will make your argument, your thesis can help you earn the two points in the Analysis & Reasoning section of the rubric (that's in addition to the one point earned in the Thesis section). To illustrate, let's look at Causation. You can earn one point for developing and supporting an argument that describes a cause/effect of a historical development/process. The second point is awarded to an argument that explains the reasons for that cause/effect. Any acceptable thesis will develop the argument, and an analytical thesis will list the reasons. So, an excellent analytical thesis will include almost everything you need for three of the six total points on the LEQ rubric.

AP World History DBQ Rubric

Like the LEQ rubric, the DBQ rubric is divided into the same four parts—**Thesis, Contextualization, Evidence,** and **Analysis & Reasoning.**

Thesis (1 point)

The DBQ thesis is constructed in the same way as that of the LEQ. You earn one point for addressing all parts of the question directly.

Contextualization (1 point)

Just as with the LEQ, the College Board® wants you to demonstrate an understanding of the historical context of your DBQ argument. Include a few statements describing the historical setting for your argument in the opening paragraph, and you will earn this point. More on this in Step 5.

Evidence (3 points)

Since the DBQ is document-based, you are rewarded for your use of the documents. You will earn one point for using the content of at least three documents to address the topic of the question. If you use at least six documents in support of your thesis, you will get a second point.

The third point is awarded for using at least one specific outside example—not a part of or from the documents—to support or qualify your argument. We will spend a good deal of time discussing evidence when we get to the body of the DBQ in Step 5.

Analysis & Reasoning (2 points)

The first of these points is awarded for a critical analysis of the sources in at least three of the documents (this used to be called Point-of-View, or POV). We will address this topic in detail as you progress through the steps of the writing process.

Just like on the LEQ, you can earn the second point of Analysis & Reasoning by demonstrating an ability to think like a professional historian by developing a complex argument utilizing the one of these historical argument techniques— *Comparison, Causation,* and *Change and Continuity Over Time* (CCOT).

Although the new rubrics are divided into distinct sections, the characteristics of any particular essay may cross over the borders of these sections. So, in theory, an essay with a clear, analytical thesis and a generally persuasive argument, but only one piece of specific evidence in support of each category, may receive the same score as an essay that contains a clear thesis that is less than analytical, but includes a very persuasive analysis of considerable evidence.

In practice, however, the essay with the stronger thesis has an advantage. The thesis is the reader's primary guide to understanding the author's argument. Consequently, on the AP exam, as in many college classes, **the thesis is viewed as a reliable predictor of the overall strength of the argument**. A weak thesis usually indicates a weak argument, whereas a clear, analytical thesis often indicates a strong argument. The reader (whether an AP scorer or college professor) is predisposed to awarding the higher score to the essay with the better thesis. It is for this reason that you should spend a good deal of time honing your thesis-writing skills.

Sample Essays for Evaluation

Now that you are familiar with the LEQ rubric and the DBQ rubric, it is time to look at some sample essays. See if you can determine why some essays are more successful than others. Read the Long Essay Question example and the three sample responses that follow it. Use the LEQ rubric guide in the previous section to help you score each essay. Be sure to evaluate the sample essay for each point-category in the rubric—Thesis, Contextualization, Evidence, and Analysis & Reasoning.

Example Question: *For centuries, Genghis (Chinggis) Khan was widely regarded as a ruthless barbarian, intent on wreaking havoc on the civilized world. Recently, however, some historians have begun to reevaluate the Mongol leader's legacy—so much so that, in 1998, the Washington Post named him, "Man of the Millennium."*

Assess this new historical interpretation. Compare and contrast the new image of Genghis (Chinggis) Khan with his longstanding historical reputation as a ruthless barbarian.

Essay #1

Genghis Khan is iconic in World History. His most brutal exploits have been documented and analyzed since the early 13th century when he and his army first emerged from the steppes of central Asia. For centuries, historians have contributed to the construct of Genghis Khan as murderous barbarian by referring back to these same documents – but this process has created an incomplete picture of a man who was so influential, the Washington Post declared him Man of the Millennium. The death and destruction wrought by the Mongol invaders is well-documented by the victims of those attacks, so even if the numbers were accurate, these accounts likely tell only part of the story. Certainly the conquered peoples had been fragmented for centuries and had experienced frequent wars among themselves long before the arrival of Genghis Khan. His actions actually put a century-long end to that constant fighting and united the continent—to the economic and cultural benefit of all its citizens. Despite the fact that Genghis (Chinggis) Khan and his army slaughtered millions of innocent people and destroyed dozens of cities and towns across Eurasia, he established a lasting peace throughout the largest empire ever conquered and reinvigorated a trade network that stretched from China to Europe.

Genghis and his army killed millions in the early 1200s, but the 12th and 13th centuries were characterized by brutality everywhere. The oppressive Jin Dynasty spent more than a hundred years tightening its grip on the various peoples of China before it was defeated by the Mongols. Seljuk and Fatimid Muslims battled each other for control of Egypt and the eastern Mediterranean, pausing only for the even more horrific Third Crusade. And when they weren't crusading, fragmented European kingdoms fought each other almost incessantly, ending the century with the start of a Hundred Years War. Additionally, the tales of "civilians lined up and slaughtered by the Mongols" were largely written by chroniclers from the defeated kingdoms. More recently, historians have suggested that many civilians who died at the hands of Genghis Khan were likely only in harms way because the defending military used them as human shields against the attacking Mongol army. Other examples of this victims' bias can be found in accounts of the Vikings. Like the Mongols, Vikings have been saddled with the reputation of ruthless barbarians, but more recent historical analysis has recast these Nordic peoples as essentially farmers and traders. Unfortunately, in both cases, centuries of historical misrepresentation were based on the overwhelming imbalance between the tomes of written accounts left by the victims in contrast with the absolute dearth of written evidence left by the attackers themselves. As for the many Mongol battles that ended in demolished cities and piles of corpses, there are as many spared cities and peoples who became Mongol vassals and lived peacefully – and with religious and cultural freedom – within the Mongol empire.

In fact, the Pax Mongolica established across Eurasia in the mid-13th century was a peace that lasted over 100 years – decades beyond the life of Genghis Khan. Conquered peoples were permitted to retain their own customs, local governments, and religious practices, so long as they remained peaceful vassals of the Mongol Empire. Recent history suggests that the Mongols were mainly interested in trade and that the Pax Mongolica was secured in order to revitalize Silk Road business. As a result of Mongol conquests, the Silk Road entered upon its Third Golden Age in the 13th century, and once again became the main route of intercontinental economic and cultural exchange.

Silk Road trade brought benefits to conquered peoples and those beyond the Mongol realm alike. Among the many ideas exchanged along the Silk Road in the 13th century were paper money and the silk production process. Travelers, like Marco Polo and Rabban bar Sauma, traveled the entire Silk Road and returned with stories of exotic foreign places further stimulating demand for imported products. The Silk Road entered into its third golden age under the control of the Mongol Empire, and the result was an economic boom that benefited peoples from Europe to China, and everywhere in between.

So the Mongols under Genghis Khan were certainly violent and brutal, but given the context of other concurrent warfare, like the Crusades, perhaps Genghis Khan's brutality was not particularly exceptional. What was exceptional for the 13th century, however, was the hundred-year Pax Mongolica established by the Mongol conquerors that led to a profusion of economic and cultural exchanges across two continents. This peaceful interaction benefited Europeans and Asians alike and spurred the final Golden Age of the Silk Road. Although it may be true that Genghis Khan and his army killed millions and decimated enemy cities, ultimately he was responsible for bringing peace to the region and, through that peace, sparking a new era of trade and cultural exchange across Eurasia.

Essay #2

Despite the fact that Genghis (Chinggis) Khan and his army slaughtered millions of innocent people and destroyed dozens of cities and towns across Eurasia, he established a lasting peace throughout the largest empire ever conquered and reinvigorated a trade network that stretched from China to Europe.

Khan and the Mongols killed many people and destroyed many cities, but it was not any worse than the rest of the violence of the century. Lots of other invaders were killing people and destroying cities. In fact, the Crusaders may have committed even more violent acts in the Holy Lands.

Also, Genghis Khan was responsible for the Pax Mongolica – the Mongol Peace. His army enforced peace all along the Silk Road, and trade expanded. Silk Road trade brought Christianity to China and silk to Italy, and all because of the Pax Mongolica.

Even though Genghis Khan killed lots of people brutally and demolished cities everywhere he went, he established peace in the end and sparked more trade along the Silk Road.

Essay #3

Genghis Khan did kill millions of people and destroy hundreds of cities, but his brutality was matched by almost every other army of his day.

Genghis and his army killed millions in the early 1200s, but the 12th and 13th centuries were characterized by brutality everywhere. The oppressive Jin Dynasty spent more than a hundred years tightening its grip on the various peoples of China before it was defeated by the Mongols. Seljuk and Fatimid Muslims battled each other for control of Egypt and the eastern Mediterranean, pausing only for the even more horrific Third Crusade. And when they weren't crusading, fragmented European kingdoms fought each other almost incessantly, ending the century with the start of a Hundred Years War. Additionally, the tales of "civilians lined up and slaughtered by the Mongols" were largely written by chroniclers from the defeated kingdoms. More recently, historians have suggested that many civilians who died at the hands of Genghis Khan were likely only in harms way because the defending military used them as human shields against the attacking Mongol army. As for the many Mongol battles that ended in demolished cities and piles of corpses, there are as many spared cities and peoples who became Mongol vassals and lived peacefully – and with religious and cultural freedom – within the Mongol empire.

Sample Essay Scores and Rationale

Now that you have evaluated and scored each of the three sample essays, review the scores and study the explanations as to why each essay received the score that it did. Then review your own answers and see how close you came to awarding the correct score.

The question is a novel variety of Comparison—the second of the College Board's History Reasoning Skills. In this example, you are being asked to compare Genghis Khan with his own reputation. Even though the question is a bit of a twist on the typical approach to C&C prompts, it is, in fact, a quite typical task in this context. Many of you have probably encountered just such an analysis in class whenever you have studied some group of nomadic invaders. Recent historical studies have forced us all to reassess the achievements and contributions of infamous warriors like the Vikings, Huns, Xiongnu, and Mongols.

So let's look at the essays.

Comments on Essay #1

Essay #1 is obviously the longest and most thorough, so how does it fare according to the rubric? The essay opens with a brief contextualization of the historical image of Genghis Khan. It alludes to the process that led to the historical construct of Khan the barbarian, and neatly sets up an assessment of that construct. Contextualization = 1 point. The thesis responds directly to the question, addressing all parts and outlining three categories of evidence in a typical 2-1 format (more on that later in the book). Although it need only appear once, this essay's opening thesis is restated in the closing paragraph as well. Thesis = 1 point. As mentioned, the categories of evidence are divided between similarities and differences – a requirement of this particular writing task. The essay begins to explain the reasons for these similarities and differences within the opening paragraph, and devotes one paragraph each to a fuller analysis of its categories of evidence. Analysis & Reasoning = 2 points. Throughout the body of the essay, several specific examples of evidence are analyzed in support of the thesis. Evidence = 2 points. Essay #1 earns all 6 points.

Comments on Essay #2

Essay #2 is much shorter, but begins with the same excellent thesis as the first essay. Thesis = 1 point. Although the body of the essay includes little specific evidence, it does describe similarities and differences and begins to explain them, at least in general terms. Analysis & Reasoning = 1 point. The inclusion of some specifics, like Crusaders, Pax Mongolica, and Silk Road, is good enough for the first evidence point. The essay fails, however, to fully analyze that evidence in support of its thesis. Evidence = 1 point. The essay makes no attempt to contextualize the argument in any way, so nothing earned in that line of the rubric. Essay #2 earns a 3.

Comments on Essay #3

Essay #3 is also short, but begins with a much weaker "thesis" than #1 and #2. In fact, since the argument in this essay includes only a single category of evidence, it fails to address all parts of the question – similarities AND differences. On the old AP rubric, this essay would earn no Thesis point whatsoever, however, since it responds to the prompt (at least partially), the new rubric awards a point. Thesis = 1 point. Without addressing BOTH similarities and differences, the essay also fails to achieve the second analysis point, awarded for demonstrating historical complexity. Analysis & Reasoning = 1 point. The essay effectively analyzes several specific examples of evidence in support of its argument, and that argument, although insufficient for the thesis point, is relevant to the question. Using Evidence = 2 points. Finally, the essay fails to contextualize the argument in any way, so no points there. Essay #3 earns a 4.

Taking the Next Step

Having reviewed and considered the sample essays, it is now time to examine and practice the process used to compose successful LEQ and DBQ essays. Begin by studying the writing process outlines that follow in the beginning of Part 2.

Part 2
The MTE Process

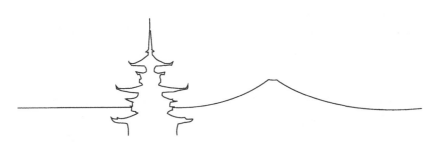

The Writing Process
—An Overview

The LEQ Writing Process

Step 1: Analyze the Question

Read the prompt and identify the tasks and terms.

Step 2: Organize the Evidence

A. Brainstorm for essential evidence.

B. Organize the evidence into categories, addressing all tasks and terms.

C. Use the categories to create an outline of your argument.

Step 3: Develop the Thesis

Create a thesis that addresses all tasks and terms of the question and uses three categories of evidence to clearly state your argument.

Step 4: Write the Opening

Draft an opening paragraph that includes the thesis and connects each category to the thesis with brief analysis (*why?* or *how?*). The opening paragraph should outline your argument and frame it within some historical context.

Step 5: Write the Body

Topic sentences from each paragraph should expand on the category statements in the opening. All evidence must relate back to the thesis (*why does this matter to the argument?*)

Step 6: Write the Closing

Close the essay by restating the opening and alluding to the best evidence from the body.

The DBQ Writing Process

Step 1: Analyze the Question

Read the prompt and identify the tasks and terms.

Step 2: Analyze the Documents

A. Read the documents, taking notes in the margin.

B. Apply the 3-Step Document Analysis process to each document:

❶ **Summarize:** What does the document say?

❷ **Analyze:** Why does the document matter to the tasks and terms?

❸ **Criticize:** How might the source affect the meaning of the document?

C. Brainstorm outside evidence to supplement the documents.

D. Group the documents and outside evidence into 3+ logical categories.

Step 3: Develop the Thesis

Create a thesis that addresses all tasks and terms of the question and uses three categories of evidence to clearly state your argument.

Step 4: Write the Opening

Draft an opening paragraph that includes the thesis and connects each category to the thesis with brief analysis (*why?* or *how?*). The opening paragraph should outline your argument and frame it within some historical context.

Step 5: Write the Body

Topic sentences from each paragraph should expand on the category statements in the opening. Analyze each (and every) document individually, as well as any specific evidence outside the document set, connecting each document and piece of evidence back to the thesis. Include source analysis (whenever possible) and document citations.

Step 6: Write the Closing

Close the essay by restating the opening and alluding to the best evidence from the body.

Analyzing the Question

When I was younger, I lived with my grandparents for a few years. I was in my first years teaching—young, single, and broke. Nanny and Pop-Pop (that's what I'd always called them, for as long as I can remember) were in their eighties—grey-haired, slower, and quite a bit shorter than they had been in their youth. I needed a cheap place to sleep and they needed a little help taking care of their three-story home. It was the perfect arrangement! I enjoyed regular home-cooked meals and clean laundry, and they had someone to do repairs, lift heavy things, and reach the little glasses on the top shelf of the cupboard.

I have many fond memories of my time with Nanny and Pop-Pop, and not-just-a-few of those memories form the basis for some of my best party bits. One incident that makes me laugh whenever I think of it involves sitting at the kitchen table with Pop while Nanny was preparing some delicious meal at the sink. This scene repeated itself three times a day, every day. Neither of my grandparents had particularly good hearing by the time I had moved in with them, so their conversations were often a bit like Abbot and Costello's "Who's on First" routine. Nanny would stand at the sink with her back to the kitchen while Pop and I were seated at the little kitchen table at the other end of the room—completely out of her sight. He might say to me, "Tony, if you have some time today, I need to go shopping." (I became Pop's chauffer after he'd given up his driver's license.) Nanny, unable to see—or hear—either one of us, but certain that Pop was saying something disparaging about her, would interject, "Now, Angelo! Tell the truth! I asked you to move those boxes last week. You said you were busy, so I moved them myself." Pop would roll his eyes at me, having heard only some of her complaint, and say, "Ruth! You can't hear a damn thing I say, can you? I don't care if you already did some shopping, the Acme has a sale on Tide and I don't want to miss it!" Nanny's retort was quick and equally disjointed, "Sure you can go for a ride, but do you have to go now? Tony's busy! Why don't you wait until later?" By this time, Pop was already standing at the door wearing his light canvas jacket and plaid newsboy cap, and running out of patience for what he considered to be Nanny's irrational nagging. "I can't wait! The sale is only today! Why can't you just mind your own business over there and give me a minute of peace!"

Although their banter was always entertaining and the memory of it still makes me chuckle, in terms of communication, it was quite ineffective. Neither one of my grandparents really understood what the other was saying (because they couldn't hear each other).

Unfortunately, my grandparents' arguments are a little like the AP exam—only not as tall. The quality of your AP essays depends largely on your clear understanding of the question. The College Board® cites misreading the question as one of the most common mistakes among AP students. Before you can develop an excellent answer, you have to be certain that you understand exactly what you've been asked to do—you must learn to analyze the tasks and terms.

TASKS: What to Do

We define TASKS as those parts of the question that tell you WHAT TO DO. The task will ask you to apply what you know about a particular period of history in a specific way. Take a look at the essay prompt below.

> **Example Question:** Compare and contrast the impact of the Black Death on China and Europe.

What is this prompt telling you to do? For this question, the tasks are "identify" and "analyze." Most AP World History essay questions identify the task with a specific verb:

Assess the extent to which cultural unity led to the expansion of ancient Eurasian states.

Discuss the arguments in favor of global cooperation to advance medical science in the 21st century.

Analyze the impact of the Industrial Revolution of the 20th century on the lower classes of China.

Some questions may require that you complete more than one task, but in every case, the question will pose your tasks explicitly.

Compare and *contrast* the influence of nationalism on Italian and German unification.

Describe and *analyze* the components of the Catholic Reformation in Spain.

Study the verbs in the sample questions above and make certain that you understand their meanings. Then, see if you can define or paraphrase each question.

assess—to understand the impact or importance of

discuss—to elaborate or explain

analyze—to explain the meaning or importance of something for something else

compare and *contrast*—to relate in terms of how one thing is like or not like another

describe—to elaborate or clarify in terms of greater detail

Make certain that you clearly understand what each one of these tasks requires you to do. Later in this book, you will learn how to respond to questions that use a slightly different format.

TERMS: What to Discuss

The TERMS of the question determine the scope of your answer. In other words, the terms are defined as those parts of the question that specify WHAT TO DISCUSS. Each question introduces a body of material that collectively forms the general subject of the essay. The terms are the words used to focus the subject of the question. These terms should elicit a body of knowledge from you that will serve as evidence later on. As you probe the terms, you should be able to start to formulate categories of evidence that will help you to develop your thesis and outline your argument.

Take a look at the example question prompt again.

> ***Example Question:*** *Compare and contrast the impact of the Black Death on China and Europe.*

What are the specific topics you are asked to address in this prompt? In this question, the terms are "impact," "Black Death," "China," and "Europe."

Taking the Next Step

Once you've analyzed the question and you understand the tasks and terms, then it's time to call upon your knowledge of history to brainstorm and organize the evidence you will need to thoroughly address the terms of the question. The way you organize your evidence will determine your categories of evidence and the foundation of your thesis. The thesis is the most important sentence in your entire essay, so anything that contributes to the quality of that sentence is something with which you must be concerned. But don't be afraid! Just turn the page and let's get to work.

Organizing the Evidence

In 1296, foundations were laid for a massive cathedral in Florence, Italy. Santa Maria del Fiore was intended to be the greatest architectural structure in all of Christendom, surpassing the great gothic cathedrals of France, Germany, and Milan. According to its original designer, Arnolfo di Cambio, the entire edifice would be crowned with a dome, the size of which would outshine even that of Santa Sophia in Europe's grandest city, Constantinople. The Commune of Florence accepted Cambio's plans, leveled forests for the necessary timber, and began floating marble down the Arno for the façade. Although Florentines agreed that the new cathedral should be, "a more beautiful and honorable temple than any in any other part of Tuscany," they understood one important problem from the outset—no one anywhere in their world of the 14th century knew how to erect a dome sufficiently large enough to cover the apse of this new cathedral. The solution would not be found until 1418—over one hundred years later—and even then, it remained untested until completion of the dome in the 1430s.

Why would a city with the resources of Florence in the 13th and 14th centuries accept a design for a structure that no one knew how to build? The answer lies in their faith—faith in the help of God and faith in the pace of innovation. They believed that God would assist them in finding someone, someday, with the knowledge and skills necessary to complete the dome, and 140 years later, their faith paid off. But wasn't that really risky? What if it had been discovered that the span of the dome was physically too large to vault and the task impossible? For starters, 140 years of building would have ended in embarrassment.

Fortunately, things turned out okay for Florence, but it took more than a century to figure out. Even still, the result could have gone the other way since no one was certain it was even possible. *Why am I telling you this?* There's a lesson to be learned here that you need to remember when writing your AP essays—don't plan an essay for which you lack the necessary skills and resources. You don't have 140 years to wait for the answer!

By mid-year in my AP class, it is not unusual for some students to write beautiful thesis statements, only to fall flat on their faces in the body of the essay because their arguments lack sufficient relevant evidence. These same students will complain that they weren't able to defend their theses because they "didn't learn enough" in order to do so. The problem these students have is not a lack of sufficient evidence to support a good thesis, but rather a thesis that fails to account for the available evidence.

As smart students learn the skills of great writing, they find it easier and easier to develop good arguments in response to any essay question. So easy, in fact, that often these very knowledgeable writers skip prewriting altogether and jump right into the essay. This is a big problem! Because brainstorming evidence is part of prewriting, skipping this part of the process means that you will begin your essay before you have gathered the necessary evidence to address the terms of the question. For example, I may know—in general terms— that Chinggis (Genghis) Khan was a military genius who used his substantial leadership skills to unify the Mongol tribes and conquer a vast empire that spanned two continents, but without specific evidence connecting his character traits to the success of the Mongols, any essay using those reasons (categories of evidence) will be relegated to broad generalizations with little support—not the best situation for an AP essay. I would do much better to begin by listing the specific evidence I actually know and then developing my categories of evidence from that list. My essay might not be the argument I wanted to make, but it will be well organized and well supported.

In this section, we will look at sample AP Long Essay Questions (LEQs). For each example, you will be asked to generate a list of specifics that you believe may be relevant to the terms of the question. You will then learn to organize your evidence into relevant categories and develop a persuasive thesis from those categories.

Right now you're probably panicking because you may feel unprepared to list specifics for all these examples. No worries! The sample questions are arranged into chronological topics that likely parallel those covered within your class, so start with whatever content you feel most comfortable. Additionally, every question is accompanied by an illustration of my own process. Although your ideas may be different, I hope my models will prove helpful. If, after all of this, you are simply blanking on some topics, *Mastering the Essay* includes a thorough list of key terms in the Appendix. Just look at the relevant time-period; the key terms should help kick-start your memory.

Brainstorming and Organizing Evidence

Too many students fail to provide enough specific, relevant evidence to adequately support their arguments. Often, their problem is not that they don't know their history, but rather that they can't think of the specific historical information necessary for their particular argument. The solution is simple—choose a different argument, one about which you know the most specific evidence. To accomplish this seemingly herculean task, you need to start with the evidence and develop the argument around it.

Identify the Tasks and Terms

As you learned in the preceding section, the first step of the process is to analyze the question by identifying the tasks and terms. Remember, we define *tasks* as those parts of the question that tell you what to do. *Terms* are defined as those parts of the question that specify the topics to be discussed in your answer.

Brainstorm Essential Evidence

Once you understand the tasks and terms, you should begin listing specific bits of history that you think might apply to the question. Brainstorm as many relevant details as you can recall that clarify or elaborate on the terms of the question. These details will serve as evidence for your essay. As you write down these pieces of evidence, you will find that the information you have written down will jog your memory further, and you will have even more evidence to use in your essay.

Organize Evidence into Categories

Once the evidence is in front of you, begin to group these bits into categories that could be applied to the tasks and terms of your question. Start by framing questions around the terms: *How are these terms connected to each other? How might this evidence help to illustrate those connections?* The questions you pose will suggest categories—themes, concepts, and characteristics—that help to demonstrate your understanding of the terms.

Develop the Thesis

Finally, using these categories, develop a working thesis and begin to formulate your opening paragraph. This may sound oversimplified, but not to worry. We will spend plenty of time delving deeper into thesis statements in the next section of this book. For now, we will focus only on organizing the evidence into effective categories.

The following example should help you better understand the process of choosing and organizing the evidence you generate through brainstorming. As I hope you will see, it is not necessary to know every detail in order to score well on the essays. You need only know how to make the best argument possible with the details that you know and understand.

Guided Practice: Brainstorming and Organizing Evidence

Directions: Read the question and identify the tasks and terms. Then, brainstorm and organize the evidence you can remember into categories that help illustrate the connections among the tasks and terms.

> **Example Question:** Analyze and assess the factors that contributed to the Mongol conquest of western Asia.

Tasks: Analyze and assess

Terms: factors, Mongol(s), conquest, western Asia

Although your memory of the Mongols may include details that are different from mine, the evidence below should help to illustrate the process. As I consider the terms individually, these are the details that come to mind:

Brainstorm Evidence:

Mongols:
Chinggis (Genghis) Khan, steppes, warriors, horses, archers, saddles, stirrups, fear, merciless, fast, nomadic, herders, yurts (gers)

Mongol conquest:
Khwarazmian Empire, Yuan Dynasty, "wrath of God", vast empire

Western Asia:
Silk Road, sparse, Taklimakan Desert, Mediterranean, Ottomans

Next, I think about the connections among the tasks and terms of the question. How did the Mongols win in western Asian battles? Who did the Mongols beat in western Asia? What role did Chinggis Khan play in the Mongol conquest? Again, my thoughts below may differ from yours, but should serve to illustrate the process:

- Mongols grew up in the Asian steppe
- The steppe was a harsh and unforgiving landscape that hardened its inhabitants
- Mongol armies traveled quickly from the Asian steppes to the Crimea
- Mongol warriors were expert archers on horseback
- Chinggis Khan had a reputation as a fierce warrior and fair leader
- Chinggis Khan united the Mongol clans for the first time in history
- Mongol enemies often lived in sedentary civilizations in the most fertile regions of Asia
- Sedentary life in fertile regions does little to prepare people for battle
- Mongols were most interested in trade and economic success
- Mongol reputation for ferocity often led to quick surrender
- Surrender to the Mongol invaders often led to a long-lasting trade relationship

These ideas were generated from the specific details brainstormed above. Now let's try to form some logical order to help address the tasks and terms of the question:

Categories of Evidence:

- Sedentary enemies were unprepared for battle with tough steppe warriors
- Chinggis Khan unified all Mongol clans
- Chinggis Khan treated his soldiers and conquered peoples fairly
- Mongols sought economic advantage through trade and battle

As we discussed earlier, these categories of evidence will form the structure of your essay. Later you will use them to construct your thesis. Remember, the thesis will tell the reader HOW you are going to answer the question. For now, here's a glimpse of one possible thesis for the example prompt using these categories.

Sample Thesis: The success of the Mongol armies in western Asia can be attributed to their **economic motivation and determination**, the **comparative strength** of Mongol warriors to their sedentary enemies, and the strength of character of their leader, **Chinggis Khan**.

We will discuss the characteristics that make this thesis effective in another section (Step 3).

Outlining an Argument

I have met many students who argue that outlining is too time-consuming, too cumbersome, and too useless to make any difference on their AP exam. These students invariably do not know how to outline an argument. Outlining should be a means to an end, not an end in itself. There is no need to use Roman numerals, parentheses, or indentations to form an outline for your argument. Think of the outline as a recipe, and the evidence as the ingredients. Organize the ingredients so that you will add them at the appropriate moments. Your outline might look like my grandmother's cookbook—circles and arrows and quick notes to yourself. Of course, it might also take a slightly more orderly form, like a chart (see "Analytical Thesis Development" in Step 3), but it will rarely look like an English assignment.

If you are still doubtful that "wasting" precious time outlining is a good idea, take another look at "Introduction to the AP Rubrics" in Part 1. You are unlikely to earn better than a 2 without a clear thesis and clear organization. Good planning enhances these characteristics, and one great way to plan your essay is by outlining. The ends justify the means.

Go back and review the Mongol conquest example above. You can identify the evidence intended for the first, second, and third categories. Use this outline to clarify for yourself how and why this evidence might be useful. Draw whatever circles, arrows, and notes that you need to plan your essay, but make sure that your outline is neat enough to follow.

Taking the Next Step

Hold up! Before we move on to Step 3, "Writing the Thesis," we need to take a look at organizing evidence for a DBQ. The process is very similar to organizing evidence for the LEQ, but made somewhat easier by the test-makers because they've given you half of the evidence! We'll need to take a look at the details of document analysis and learn to effectively combine the evidence given by the DBQ with our own memory of history.

Analyzing the Documents

Although most students are a little afraid of the AP World History DBQ, my students come to absolutely love that section of the exam. Think about it—half of the evidence is provided for you, the tasks and terms are no more difficult than those in the Long Essay Questions, and the points in the rubric are essentially a checklist. What's not to like?

The real challenge to writing a great DBQ essay is understanding the documents used in the question. With some practice, this too will pose no real problem. Like the LEQ, you begin the DBQ by breaking down the question into its tasks and terms. Then, instead of brainstorming evidence, simply start reading the documents. As you read each one, think about the ways it might be used to address the tasks and terms of the question. Write notes next to each document to help you remember what you were thinking when you read it. You should also think about each document's origin, purpose, and author while you read it. Later on, we will talk more in-depth about these three elements when the process of document analysis is introduced.

As you go through this process, you will probably remember additional specific evidence that might be useful in your essay. List these other details as you did for the LEQ. When you identify specific groups of documents and other evidence that can be used to support your thesis, make notes about that, too. As you develop these categories of evidence, you should also begin to see a thesis developing. Write down your ideas about this thesis, as well. Eventually, you will have generated an informal outline like those from Step 2 (LEQ), and then you will be ready to begin writing your essay.

The test-makers give you 15 minutes to prewrite for your DBQ, but don't worry if you haven't yet finished analyzing documents and brainstorming evidence after this assigned reading period. You can continue to prewrite even after the proctor distributes the essay booklets. Remember, the rubric rewards clarity and organization, so even if it takes 20–25 minutes to prepare your DBQ outline, you will have enough time to finish writing—and your essay will be better for the effort. Now let's look at the process, step by step, just like we did for the LEQ.

Document Analysis—Getting Started

To better understand how to analyze the documents in a DBQ, let's take look at an example DBQ prompt and practice document.

Example Question: *Analyze and assess the factors contributing to the victory of Chinese Communism over the Kuomintang in 1949.*

As always, we first identify the tasks and terms of the question.

Tasks: Analyze AND Assess

Terms: contributing factors, victory, Chinese Communists, Kuomintang, 1949

Now let's analyze the document together.

Document A

SOURCE: Mao Zedong, Communist Party leader, from his concluding speech at the Seventh National Congress of the Communist Party of China, 11 June 1945

…We should fire the whole people with the conviction that China belongs not to the reactionaries but to the Chinese people. There is an ancient Chinese fable called "The Foolish Old Man Who Removed the Mountains". It tells of an old man who lived in northern China long, long ago and was known as the Foolish Old Man of North Mountain. His house faced south and beyond his doorway stood the two great peaks, Taihang and Wangwu, obstructing the way. He called his sons, and hoe in hand they began to dig up these mountains with great determination. Another graybeard, known as the Wise Old Man, saw them and said derisively, "How silly of you to do this! It is quite impossible for you few to dig up those two huge mountains." The Foolish Old Man replied, "When I die, my sons will carry on; when they die, there will be my grandsons, and then their sons and grandsons, and so on to infinity. High as they are, the mountains cannot grow any higher and with every bit we dig, they will be that much lower. Why can't we clear them away?" Having refuted the Wise Old Man's wrong view, he went on digging every day, unshaken in his conviction. God was moved by this, and he sent down two angels, who carried the mountains away on their backs. Today, two big mountains lie like a dead weight on the Chinese people. One is imperialism, the other is feudalism. The Chinese Communist Party has long made up its mind to dig them up. We must persevere and work unceasingly, and we, too, will touch God's heart. Our God is none other than the masses of the Chinese people. If they stand up and dig together with us, why can't these two mountains be cleared away?

What does the document say about the Chinese Communists and/ or the Kuomintang?

The document describes a united party that is determined to defeat the foreign and domestic forces working against them. The author uses positive language when speaking of the Communist Party, such as unity and light. He also uses an ancient Chinese parable to make a point about persistence and unity. The document says nothing of the Kuomintang directly, however, if "imperialism" implies foreign influence, then "feudalism" might imply the current Kuomintang rulers.

Why is the document important to our understanding of HOW or WHY the Chinese Communists defeated the Kuomintang?

The document supports the argument that the Communists were determined and united with the people of China. It also illustrates some of the techniques used by Mao Zedong to gain support for communism among the people of China, including his employment of old familiar Chinese parables in support of very new and unfamiliar political ideals.

What do you know about the source of the document? How might the source have affected the meaning of the document?

Mao Zedong was to be the leader of the Peoples Republic of China after the defeat of the Kuomintang in 1949. He had been an important Communist leader in China since the 1920's, and was instrumental in shaping party policy throughout that period. The source line indicates that this was Mao's final speech at the conclusion of the Seventh National Congress of the Communist Party and that it took place on 11 June 1945.

We can surmise, even if we had not known before, that Mao Zedong is an important character in the Chinese Communist Party from the fact that he delivered the concluding speech at the party's National Congress. From this, it is possible to say that this speech will be widely disseminated and is likely to have great impact on the future of the Communist movement in China. The date of the speech helps us to further contextualize the speech. By June 1945, Japan was retreating from central China and only two months from defeat at the hands of the United States and its allies in the Pacific. Since Japanese aggression in China during WWII was particularly brutal, Mao's determination to rid China of "imperialism" was probably very well received.

That's it! I know, I know—you're sitting there thinking, "What's it?" How do you know what questions to ask? How do you know if your answers are correct? How do you finish all this pre-essay work in just a few minutes? How does all this help to write a DBQ essay on the AP World exam? Take a breath. Now read on and let's look at the fundamentals of document analysis.

The 3-Step Document Analysis Process

Document analysis can be a scary process, especially when it's presented as a seemingly random list of questions—like those in the previous section. If we look at the essence of document analysis, however, it really boils down to three very reasonable steps—**Summarize, Analyze, Criticize**. To better understand the logic behind this 3-Step Process, imagine that you are a spectator at a Final Four basketball game. The game is tight in the closing minutes and someone a few rows away yells something directly at you, but you didn't quite hear what they said. What do you do? First, and most importantly, you ask, "What did you say?" You can do nothing before you know what was said. Then, as you interpret the meaning of the words, you ask yourself, "Why does this matter to me?" Maybe the person yelled, "Do you want a hotdog?" It's the end of the game, so those words may not matter. But maybe the person yelled, "Your hair is on fire!" That might matter more. Finally, as you decode the significance of the words, you account for the speaker. Who is this person and why is he talking to me? Might there be some other meaning to these words in this context?

The **3-Step Process** is just like that basketball game. When you approach a document for the first time, you have to ask, "What does it say?" This is step 1 – **Summarize**. Once you understand the document, you have to decide, "Why does it matter?" This is step 2 – **Analyze**. Finally, you have to consider the source. "How might this source have influenced the meaning of this document?" This is step 3 – **Criticize**.

Now try to follow these steps as you go through the example exercise below.

Guided Practice: Using the 3-Step Process to Analyze Documents for the DBQ

Directions: Identify the tasks and terms in the following question, and then use the 3-Step Process to determine how each document might address those tasks and terms. Write your notes in the margins. As you analyze the documents, make a list of other specific evidence that comes to mind.

> **Exercise Question:** To what extent did the long-standing disputes between Eastern and Western Christendom contribute to the fall of Constantinople in 1453?

Document A

SOURCE: Pope Gregory VII in a letter written to Ebouly de Rossi, 1073

It is far better for a country to remain under the rule of Islam than be governed by Christians who refuse to acknowledge the rights of the Catholic Church.

Document B

SOURCE: St. Mark Eugenicus, 15th-century Greek Orthodox theologian

Flee from the papists as you would from a snake and from the flames of a fire.

Document C

> SOURCE: **Pope Nicholas V to Constantine XI (Byzantine Emperor), 1452**
>
> If you, with your nobles and the people of Constantinople accept the decree of union, you will find Us and Our venerable brothers, the cardinals of the Holy Roman Church, ever eager to support your honor and your empire. But if you and your people refuse to accept the decree, you will force Us to take such measures as are necessary for your salvation and Our honor.

Document D

> SOURCE: **George of Hungary, prisoner of the Ottomans 1436-1458, written c. 1453**
>
> When recruiting for the army is begun, they gather with such readiness and speed you might think they are invited to a wedding not a war... those left at home feel an injustice has been done to them. They claim they will be happier if they die on the battlefield among the spears and arrows of the enemy than at home....

Document E

> SOURCE: **Chalcocondylas, Byzantine chronicler on the Ottoman soldiers, 1453**
>
> There is no prince who has his armies and camps in better order, both in abundance of victuals and in the beautiful order they use in encamping without any confusion or embarrassment.

Document F

SOURCE: **Leonard of Chios, Genoese archbishop of Mytilene, letter to Pope Nicholas V, 1453**

I can testify that Greeks, Latins, Germans, Hungarians, Bohemians and men from all the Christian countries were on the side of the Turks ... Oh, the wickedness of denying Christ like this!

Document G

SOURCE: **George Sphrantzes, *The Fall of the Byzantine Empire: A Chronicle*, written c. 1470**

The emperor consented to have the pope's name commemorated in our services, by necessity, as we hoped to receive some aid. Whoever were willing would pronounce the commemoration in Saint Sophia; the rest would incur no blame and remain peaceful. These services took place on November 12. Six months later we had received as much aid from Rome as had been sent to us by the sultan of Cairo.

Explanation

So let's see how well you did.

For each document, you should have begun with **Summarize** by asking, "What does it say?" Then, **Analyze** by asking, "Why does it matter (to the tasks and terms of the question)?" (For example, What does each document say about the "long-standing disputes between Eastern and Western Christendom" or the "fall of Constantinople in 1453"? Does the document state or imply anything about HOW the disputes may have contributed to the fall?) Finally, **Criticize** by asking, "What do I know about this source and how might it have influenced the meaning of this document?"

Document A

SUMMARIZE – Pope Gregory would prefer that the Eastern Christians remain under Islamic control if they refuse to submit to Rome.

ANALYZE – As early as 1073, the East/West disputes seem to influence the pope's attitude about the Byzantine struggle against the Ottomans.

CRITICIZE – As leader of the Western Church at the time of the Great Schism, Pope Gregory may be trying to pressure Easterners to rejoin Rome.

Document B

SUMMARIZE – St. Mark compares the threat of the Roman Church to that of a snake or a fire.

ANALYZE – In the 1400s, the East/West disputes continue to be contentious.

CRITICIZE – As an Orthodox theologian, St. Mark's views may exemplify a wider view among Easterners.

Document C

SUMMARIZE – Pope Nicholas V poses reunification with Rome as a prerequisite for Western help in Constantinople.

ANALYZE – East/West disputes are apparently a significant barrier to cooperation, even in the face of Ottoman threats.

CRITICIZE – Nicholas, as pope, still holds the views of his predecessors of four centuries earlier.

Document D

SUMMARIZE – George of Hungary speaks well of the bravery of Ottoman soldiers.

ANALYZE – This document says nothing directly about the East/West disputes, but does lend credence to an alternative reason for the fall of Constantinople—Ottoman bravery.

CRITICIZE – A prisoner from the opposing army is unlikely to speak well of his enemy unless he was very impressed.

Document E

SUMMARIZE – Chalcondylas speaks well of the Ottoman army.

ANALYZE – This document supports an alternative reason for the fall of Constantinople, the strength of the Ottoman army.

CRITICIZE – Although his loyalty to the emperor is uncertain from the description "Byzantine chronicler," it is likely that Chalcocondylas would not overstate his praise of the enemy unless he was very impressed. In combination with Document D, this evidence is even stronger.

Document F

SUMMARIZE – Leonard of Chios says that Westerners helped the Ottoman army in the siege of Constantinople. He compares their assistance to denying Christ.

ANALYZE – Implies that the East/West disputes were more important than defending Christianity in 1453, and the disputes led to increased Ottoman military strength through direct assistance from the West.

CRITICIZE – A Roman Catholic bishop writing to the pope is unlikely to speak offensively. Because he described the Western help as "denying Christ," it may be that, at least officially, the pope would be unwilling to accept East/West disputes as justification for helping the infidel.

Document G

SUMMARIZE – Sphrantzes writes that the emperor agreed to commemorate the pope in religious services in Constantinople, presumably in exchange for help from the West, but no help ever came. He implies that the emperor acted honorably.

ANALYZE – Although the document makes no mention of the East/ West disputes, it can be used to support the contention that the actions of the West contributed to the fall of Constantinople, no matter what the root cause of those actions may have been.

CRITICIZE – Sphrantzes, although not cited as such, can be assumed to be Byzantine based on his use of the first-person in the chronicle. This may help to explain his criticism of the West.

DBQ Categories of Evidence

Just as with the LEQ, your DBQ argument should be divided into three logical categories of evidence. The task is a bit easier with the DBQ because most of the evidence has been provided for you in the form of the documents. As you analyze the documents and brainstorm outside evidence, you should begin to see how some of it might be used to support a thesis.

In the example above, Documents A and B are both evidence of the intensity of the long-standing distrust and animosity between the churches of the East and the West. Documents C, F, and G attest to the fact that the Western Church may have used the Ottoman threat to gain some control over the Eastern Church. Documents D and E, on the other hand, lend credence to a counter argument that Mehmet's army was simply better than that of the Byzantines. Additional outside evidence might include specifics of the Great Schism, details of Venetian actions in the months leading up to the Fall of Constantinople, or further support for the strength and preparedness of the Ottoman army. So an outline of three logical categories might look like this:

The intensity of the East/West dispute

> Docs A and B

> Other specific evidence of the Great Schism

The West's use of the crisis to regain control of the East

> Docs C, F, and G

Details of Venetian actions in the months leading up to the fall of Constantinople

The strength of the Ottoman army

Docs D and E

Other specific evidence of the strength and preparedness of the Ottoman army

Taking the Next Step

Now that you have analyzed the documents, brainstormed some outside evidence, and grouped everything into three logical categories of evidence, you should have no trouble developing a thesis and writing the opening paragraph. Since the thesis is such a critical piece of the essay, we will spend the next section of the book honing your thesis skills.

Constructing the Thesis

Ever wonder what a bunch of history teachers would talk about in their spare time? Probably not. But if you're even a little bit curious, when AP Readers are thrown together every year to score the exam essays, they spend a good bit of their time talking about thesis statements. Okay, maybe not so much "talking about" as "lamenting the absence of."

Select teachers and professors of history are brought together every year by the wonderful people who produce the AP exams—the College Board®. Some of our families refer to the gathering as summer camp for history geeks. And although each year brings its own unique topics of conversation, one consistent theme is the thesis. Readers continually lament the apparent lack of thesis writing skills among AP History students.

Many of us teach AP History ourselves, so we know our students are writing good thesis statements. What we wonder is why so many other students are unable to do the same. This question was one of the biggest reasons why I set out to write *Mastering the Essay*. I decided to share what I do in class within the pages of this book because I know that learning to write consistently good thesis statements is an utterly doable task for any student.

This unit will guide you through a process that my own students have followed for years with great results. First, we will identify the elements of a great thesis, and then you will learn to construct a variety of thesis types. At the end of the unit, you will be ready to respond to any AP World History question with a clear, analytical thesis worthy of a top score on the AP rubric.

The Art of the Thesis

As you read earlier in this text (several times), the thesis is the single most important part of the essay. AP World History Readers consistently say that the thesis is "the heart of the essay." If the thesis is strong, the essay is likely to be strong, as well. If the thesis is weak, the essay is probably weak, too.

If they're not still fresh in your mind, take a minute to review the first two steps of the process. Once again, start with the tasks of the question—what are you asked to do? Next, identify the terms of the question—what are you asked to discuss?

A good thesis attacks the tasks and terms head-on. Respond to the question directly by telling the reader why and/or how you will complete the tasks within the body of your essay by using the terms. Your thesis must address the terms of the question explicitly and directly, and outline, however briefly, the categories of evidence you will use to make your point. Although it is not absolutely necessary to use three categories of evidence in every essay, it is a good rule of thumb. This is why so many English teachers refer to thesis essays as 5-paragraph essays—one opening paragraph, three body paragraphs (one for each category of evidence), and one closing paragraph.

Next, let's review the categories of evidence we created for the example prompt in Step 2 (LEQ).

> **Example Question:** *Analyze and assess the factors that contributed to the Mongol conquest of western Asia.*

Tasks: Analyze and assess

Terms: factors, Mongol(s), conquest, western Asia

Categories of Evidence:

- Sedentary enemies were unprepared for battle with tough steppe warriors
- Chinggis Khan unified all Mongol clans
- Chinggis Khan treated his soldiers and conquered peoples fairly

- Mongols sought economic advantage through trade and battle

As we discussed earlier, these categories of evidence will form the structure of your essay. Use them to construct your thesis. Remember, the thesis will tell the reader HOW you are going to answer the question. Take another look at one possible thesis for the example prompt.

> **Sample Thesis:** The success of the Mongol armies in western Asia can be attributed to their **economic motivation and determination**, the **comparative strength** of Mongol warriors to their sedentary enemies, and the strength of character of their leader, **Chinggis Khan**.

As you can see, this thesis effectively states how you are going to answer the question and outlines the argument you will make in the body of the essay.

Developing a successful thesis is integrally connected to how carefully you read and how clearly you understand the tasks and terms of the essay question. For that reason, the exercises for each of the following sections are grounded in sample essay questions. These sets of exercises are designed to help you master the art of creating a successful thesis. The first section provides a series of examples of theses and asks you to identify how each would score on an AP exam. The second set of exercises asks you to generate a successful thesis based upon the process that you just learned. As you complete each set of exercises, remember that you are building on a process that will help you to compose clear, analytical thesis statements and consistently successful essays.

In order to write an excellent thesis, it helps to know what one looks like. The exercise below contains a sample essay question followed by several possible thesis responses. Your job is to score each thesis statement according to the criteria outlined in the LEQ rubric. Before you begin, review the LEQ rubric guide on page 7 of Part 1 to familiarize yourself with the thesis qualities that correspond with each score.

Guided Practice: Thesis Recognition

Directions: Begin each exercise in this set by identifying the tasks and terms of the question (**Step 1**). Next, read the thesis statements below the question. Then, on the line beside each thesis, provide the score that you think it deserves. Since the rubric awards one point for an acceptable thesis and you can move toward an additional point for Analysis & Reasoning by outlining your argument with an analytical thesis, you should rate each thesis with a 0, 1, or 1+ (for a strong analytical thesis).

Follow along with the sample exercise below to see how it's done. The sample exercise is followed by answers and explanations to illustrate the process.

> **Exercise Question:** Compare and contrast the impact of geography on the political, economic, and belief systems of ancient Egypt and Mesopotamia.

Tasks: Compare, contrast

Terms: Geography; political, economic, and belief systems; Egypt and Mesopotamia

Possible Thesis Statement Responses:

_____ **A.** The Nile River and the Fertile Crescent were similar because, in both cases, their locations in fertile river valleys supported great agricultural economies and governments rooted in religion.

_____ **B.** Although both economies were rooted in the agriculture of fertile river valleys, the predictability of the Nile, coupled with Egypt's natural boundaries, promoted stable governments and a deeply rooted belief system, while the irregularity of the Tigris and Euphrates, as well as a lack of natural boundaries, helped to produce unstable governments and changing belief systems.

_____ **C.** Geography impacted Egypt and Mesopotamia in many ways.

_____ **D.** Geography impacted Egypt and Mesopotamia politically, economically, and religiously.

_____ **E.** Despite the similarities of economies within fertile river valleys, Egypt differed from Mesopotamia because the Nile was predictable while the Tigris and Euphrates were unpredictable.

_____ **F.** Both river valleys produced agricultural economies, however, Egypt generated a stable government and belief system based on the Nile, while Mesopotamia's governments and religions were less stable.

_____ **G.** While Egypt's Nile River flooded at regular intervals and across predictable areas, the Tigris and Euphrates of Mesopotamia flooded much more irregularly and unpredictably, however both civilizations produced agricultural economies.

Explanation

A. **(1 point)** This thesis connects the geography of each kingdom to its economy, government, and religion. There is even a bit of analysis in so far as the river valleys are described as fertile. The question asks for the completion of two tasks—compare AND contrast—but this thesis only compares. The old rubric would have awarded zero points for this mistake, but the new rubric allows students to earn the Thesis point for any claim that responds to the prompt.

B. **(1+ points)** This thesis outlines the similarities and differences (both tasks), addresses each of the terms of the question by speaking to the governments, economies, and belief systems of the two kingdoms, and connects its categories of evidence to its main premise with some basic WHYs and HOWs. It satisfies all the basic requirements of an acceptable thesis and enhances those with analysis.

C. **(0 points)** This is a simple restatement of the question.

D. **(0 points)** Although this seems to go beyond a simple restatement of the prompt, the "categories of evidence" are so vague that they add nothing to the author's point. Additionally, AP readers see so many essays that begin in this generic fashion, that this type of opening signals a weak and unsophisticated essay.

E. **(1 point)** This thesis satisfies all the basic requirements of an acceptable thesis, but lacks any analysis. Although it notes the geography of the river valleys, and outlines the similarities and differences, it fails to connect those terms by describing WHY or HOW the geography helped to create the government, economy, or belief system.

F. **(1 point)** This is very similar to Example E. While satisfying the basic requirements, it fails to offer any analysis.

G. **(1 point)** Again, this is similar to Example E. The author notes the geographies of the river valleys, even pointing to specific details (regular vs. irregular flooding), but has failed to explicitly connect the geography to political and belief systems.

Analytical Thesis Development

In the exercise above, we alluded to the connection between an analytical thesis and the points for Analysis & Reasoning. *So what makes a thesis analytical anyway?* If you think of your thesis as the WHAT of your response, and your categories of evidence as the HOW of your response, then you can think of analysis as the WHY these categories matter to the thesis. After just this one sentence, the reader understands WHAT you intend to say, HOW you intend to say it, and WHY you have chosen to say it in this particular way. Yes, one sentence can do all that! That's a strong thesis.

So, once again, a strong essay begins with a strong thesis, and the strength of a thesis is determined by the ways in which it addresses the tasks and terms of the question. Once you have identified the tasks and terms of the question, brainstormed a list of essential evidence, and grouped your evidence into three logical categories, you are ready to develop an analytical thesis. To do this, you must decide how best to complete the tasks using the evidence available to you.

In the following example, the task is written as "to what extent." While it does not use a specific verb like most essay questions, this is still a common question format. Unfortunately, the misinterpretations of it are equally common. Many of the incorrect ways to answer this question include the phrase "to a great extent." The "to what extent" question is not asking "how much," but rather "how." The question may be rephrased as "in what ways is the relationship true and in what ways is it false?" Like a "compare & contrast" essay, the best "to what extent" answers should develop categories of evidence to demonstrate the truth of the relationship (compare), and categories to show that it may be false (contrast).

> **Exercise Question:** *To what extent does the increasing popularity of World Cup soccer reflect the overall globalization of the world in the late 20th and early 21st centuries?*

Tasks: To what extent (In what ways is this true? AND In what ways is this false?)

Terms: Popularity, World Cup soccer, and globalization

Question Restated: In what ways does the increasing popularity of World Cup soccer reflect the overall globalization of the world in the late 20th and early 21st centuries? In what ways does the increasing popularity of World Cup soccer NOT reflect the overall globalization of the world in the late 20th and early 21st centuries?

One way to complete this task is to identify specific characteristics of the increasing popularity of World Cup soccer, and then to show whether or not those characteristics share some commonalities with the characteristics of the overall globalization. Below you can see a brief list of some characteristics of World Cup soccer that you might have brainstormed in response to this question. Next to the list are some characteristics of globalization.

Characteristics of World Cup Soccer	Characteristics of Overall Globalization
Worldwide media coverage	Expanded international communication networks
Greater levels of international participation	Expanded international transportation networks
Increased merchandising of World Cup teams	Fewer restrictions to cross-border trade
World spotlight on host nation	Widespread sharing of ideas
Rising level of play among competitors	

The challenge now is to make sense of the information in terms of the question. As you learned in Step 1, start to pose questions that link the terms with the question. When answering an "in what ways" or a "to what extent" question, it is often a good idea to categorize your evidence according to the "ways."

In what ways is the increasing popularity of World Cup soccer like globalization?

- Level of play is improved by "sharing of ideas" among competitors

- Expanded media coverage allows for greater fan participation worldwide

- International merchandising breaks down barriers to fan participation

In what ways is the increasing popularity of World Cup soccer NOT like globalization?

- Fan base is primarily local and nationalistic

So, the relationship is true in terms of sharing of ideas, media coverage, and international merchandising, but is false in terms of the sense of nationalism of the local fan base. This is enough for a working thesis.

Thesis: To the extent that the popularity of the World Cup has grown through shared ideas, expanded media coverage, and international merchandising, it reflects the overall process of globalization; however, to the extent that most of a team's fan base is localized within its borders and heavily nationalistic, World Cup soccer does not reflect the process of globalization.

Guided Practice: Analytical Thesis Development

Directions: For each of the exercises in this set, follow the model you have learned to develop a thesis that answers the question. Be sure to complete each step of the prewriting process to insure that your response is well organized.

Step 1: Identify the tasks and terms

Step 2: Restate the question, and then create a chart to organize the ideas you brainstorm.

Finally, craft your analytical thesis statement.

> **Exercise Question:** Analyze the impact of the Ottoman expansion into Europe on European politics and society, 1453–1600.

Explanation

Now compare your response to the sample response shown below. In order to be correct, your thesis does not need to be identical to the one that follows. Look for common characteristics that your thesis and the sample thesis share. Did you address the tasks fully? Did you include the terms? Did you organize your thesis around the HOWs or WHYs of the question? Did you imply clear categories of evidence?

Tasks: Analyze

Terms: Impact of the Ottoman expansion, European politics and society, 1453–1600

Question Restated: In what ways or for what reasons were European politics and society affected by the rise of the Ottomans between 1453 and 1600?

The web that follows is the result of brainstorming and organizing. At first, the details inside the white bubbles were just a list of evidence. As I began to look for logical groups, I developed the ideas in the black bubbles and grouped my brainstormed evidence accordingly. If you look at the resulting web, you can see that all the evidence connected with the fall of Constantinople helped to reinforce the Church split. The ongoing struggles between the West and the Ottomans in the period from Mehmet to Suleiman, meanwhile, led to the decline of the Venetians and the rise of the Hapsburgs.

Sample Chart:

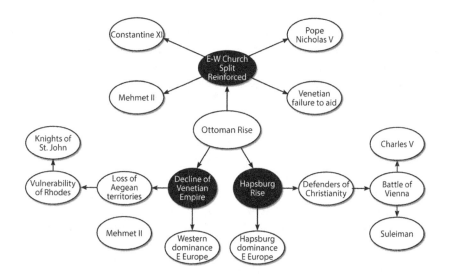

Compare the sample thesis with the web above.

Sample Thesis: The Ottoman expansion into Europe directly impacted European politics by elevating the Hapsburgs <u>who fought to repel them</u> and diminishing the Venetians <u>who needed free access to the sea for trade</u>; and, by causing the fall of Constantinople, impacted European society through a heightened sense of mutual distrust <u>that helped to calcify the East-West split in the Christian churches</u>.

You should recognize each of the three categories of evidence as the ideas in the black bubbles around which the evidence is organized. The italicized phrases serve as analysis because they demonstrate why each category matters to this thesis. If your prewriting has produced something similar to the chart and thesis above, your essay is practically written for you.

Taking the Next Step

Remember, the structure of a thesis depends upon the categories of evidence that you have brainstormed. Review your answers for this section and take note of how you used those categories to construct your analytical thesis statements. Now you need to practice explaining the significance of those categories of evidence in your opening paragraph.

4

Writing the
Opening Paragraph

For years, I've delivered a consistently harsh and loud message to my AP History students. Whenever they would begin an essay with mounds of fluffy narrative that English teachers might call setting, I would cut them off at the knees with a sharp, "Answer the stinkin' question!" For 16 years the AP World History FRQ and DBQ rubrics rewarded clarity and directness—no points for setting. Students often get lost in their own text when they try to set the stage for an answer that even they don't fully understand yet, so banning setting altogether usually resulted in better—and higher scoring—essays. But now, some things have changed.

The newest AP World History LEQ and DBQ essay rubrics now reward setting—*if you do it well*. It is still a terrible idea to begin your essay with a page of directionless fluff that you hope will end in an acceptable thesis. A well-planned, purposeful setting that establishes the historical context of your argument, however, followed by a clear and direct answer to the question prompt, will definitely boost your score. More specifically, a thoughtful statement of setting at the start of your essay might be the best way to earn the point for Contextualization.

The Contextualization point is earned by explaining the broader context within which your argument is best understood. Sometimes this context is a series of events or an historical era, but it may also be an historical theme or process. In any case, situating your argument within its broader context is now a great idea when writing AP essays. And the best place to contextualize your argument is probably within the opening paragraph in the form of a well-structured setting.

So feel free to indulge your English teacher on the new AP World History essays, and create a few sentences that set the stage for your argument. Then... answer the stinkin' question!

Planning a Strong Opening

As with so many other components of good essays, there is really no absolutely correct way to develop your opening paragraph. Since clarity and directness are rewarded on both AP essay rubrics, we will develop a process that leads to a clear and direct opening paragraph.

For the sake of directness, don't spend *too much* space on setting in your essays. Although establishing the historical context for your answer is a great writing technique, too often students get lost in the setting and don't get to their thesis until page two. Instead, develop two to four sentences that can explain the historical "environment" within which your argument makes the most sense. Then write your thesis, and continue with your opening paragraph.

In the thesis, you addressed the tasks and terms of the question by stating explicitly WHAT you believe to be the answer to the question. You also outlined your three categories of evidence, which tell the reader HOW you intend to answer the question. If the thesis contains the answer to the question and all three categories of evidence, what are you going to write in the other sentences of the first paragraph? First, it should be noted that style and paragraph form are not assessed on the AP World History essay rubrics. So, if you write only the thesis in the opening paragraph, you will not be penalized. However, your essay will be well served if you develop your opening paragraph to state WHY your categories matter to your thesis—the same question you began to answer in your analytical thesis. One way to address this point is to write separate sentences for each category of evidence, answering briefly in each case, "Why does this matter to my thesis?"

Guided Practice: Presenting the Argument

Directions: For this set of exercises, you will practice all the skills covered so far in this book:

Step 1: Identify the tasks and terms

Step 2: Brainstorm specific evidence

Step 3: Develop a thesis and categories of evidence, and then outline your argument

Next, using the strategies outlined in the section above, write an opening paragraph for each thesis statement. The example below asks you to write an opening paragraph for the sample thesis shown, and is followed by a model solution to help you better understand the goal of this exercise.

Exercise Question: *Compare and contrast the impact of geography on the political, economic, and belief systems of ancient Egypt and Mesopotamia.*

Sample Thesis: Although both economies were rooted in the agriculture of fertile river valleys, the predictability of the Nile, coupled with Egypt's natural boundaries, promoted stable governments and a deeply rooted belief system, while the irregularity of the Tigris and Euphrates, as well as a lack of natural boundaries, helped to produce unstable governments and changing belief systems.

Explanation

Sample Opening Paragraph: The nomadic peoples of the eastern Mediterranean survived for millennia in lands dominated by hot desert climates. They became adept at hunting and gathering in some of the most inhospitable regions of the world, and their ultimate success relied largely on taking advantage of relatively small fertile areas along the few rivers they encountered. It was the development of agriculture along these river valleys that resulted in two of the most prosperous centers of civilization in the world—Egypt and Mesopotamia. River valleys, like those in Egypt and Mesopotamia, were ideal locations for ancient farming communities to grow into long-lasting civilizations, because river flooding provided a constant source of fertile farmland in an otherwise harsh environment. Both civilizations benefitted to some degree from fertile farmland, but the precise location of each river valley and the particular nature of each river led to distinctions in terms of the political and economic stability of each particular civilization. Although both economies were rooted in the agriculture of fertile river valleys, the predictability of the Nile, coupled with Egypt's natural boundaries, promoted stable governments and a deeply rooted belief system, while the irregularity of the Tigris and Euphrates, as well as a lack of natural boundaries, helped to produce unstable governments and changing belief systems in Mesopotamia.

The opening begins with a brief description of life in the lands of the eastern Mediterranean, describing the harsh climate and desert conditions endured by the nomadic peoples of western Asia and northern Africa. These few sentences set your reader up for the contrast of the more settled lifestyles of the river valley peoples. In the thesis—located at the end of the paragraph—we tell the reader that both Egypt and Mesopotamia benefitted from their locations in river valleys, but that the nature of those valleys influenced the specific outcomes. We also say HOW the essay will illustrate this point—through a comparison of fertile farmlands, predictability of floods, and natural boundaries. The sentences preceding the thesis explain briefly WHY our three categories of evidence help to distinguish between the civilizations of ancient Egypt and those of ancient Mesopotamia. Some restatement of each of these sentences could be used as topic sentences for our body paragraphs, but we'll save that discussion for Step 5.

Taking the Next Step

Having completed your opening paragraph, you will have clearly told your reader WHAT you think is the answer to the question and HOW you will present the details of your argument. Once you've created this sturdy skeleton of an argument, now it's time to put some meat on the bones. In the next section, you will learn the best way to introduce specific evidence in the body of your essay, and how to best use that evidence in support of your thesis.

Writing the Body

I'm an idea guy—a big picture thinker. I happily go through each day brainstorming new and exciting ideas, often one after the next—some good, some not. Once, after a particularly rainy day at a campground, my friend, Bob (another idea guy), and I sat outside my RV with our feet in the mud, doing our best to enjoy the evening. Eventually, we both found ourselves staring across the road at a beat-up, old trailer with the intelligent addition of a small, wooden deck outside the front door. Meanwhile, there we sat, outside a brand new, fancy RV, with soaking wet shoes and muddy pant legs. Bob and I agreed that there was definitely a problem that needed to be addressed.

So that night we came up with a solution—a portable aluminum deck that we could disassemble and bring with us on all our RV camping trips. We were certain that it was a great idea, but we also understood that as long as it remained just an idea, we still had wet shoes. At some point, even idea guys have to get down to the work of fleshing out the details. So, we spent the next two years designing, testing, redesigning, and prototyping our solution. In the end, our idea became a reality—the Porta-Deck.

It's the same for your essay. By now you are likely very tired of all my harping on the benefits of thorough prewriting, and of course, it is your prewriting that allows you to more easily progress through the rest of the steps of writing a top-scoring AP World History LEQ or DBQ. But at some point in the process, your essay needs its details. It's time to get your feet out of the mud and write some body paragraphs.

Introduction to the Body Paragraph

In Step 2, we discussed evidence analysis as it applies to the prewriting phase of your essays. Now we have to address the writing phase. Even though your essay will benefit most from a clear argument and good organization—elements developed in your prewriting—you now have to actually write your essay.

Look back at the overview of the LEQ rubric guide on page 7 in Part 1 and you will see that—in order to earn even 1 of the 2 points in the Evidence section—you must support your thesis with *"specific* examples of *relevant* evidence." The inclusion of evidence is necessary, but not sufficient for the best LEQ responses. To earn the second Evidence point and have a chance at the top score, you have to explicitly analyze your evidence to "support" your thesis.

The easiest way to remember to analyze your evidence explicitly within the body of your essay is to continually ask yourself, "Why does this matter to my thesis?" Your answer to that question is the analysis required in your body paragraphs. Remember, as part of your prewriting, you developed categories of evidence—themes, concepts, and characteristics—that relate to the specifics of the essay question. Remember also that you used those categories of evidence to structure your thesis and, by extension, your essay as a whole. Now you are providing specific pieces of evidence that clarify or explain those categories. Every time you introduce new evidence, follow it with an explanation as to how it relates to that category of evidence. This will explain why it matters to your thesis.

Each body paragraph should be comprised of:

1. A topic sentence that states why this category of evidence matters to your thesis (Remember, your thesis is structured according to the categories of evidence you have chosen to answer the essay question.)

2. Sentences describing each specific piece of evidence (for example, a specific aspect of a time period or event)

3. Sentences analyzing why each piece of evidence develops a category of evidence, and therefore, matters to your thesis

If you have developed three categories of evidence—which should always be your goal—then you will end up with three body paragraphs. The following exercises are meant to use those skills for LEQs and DBQs.

Guided Practice: Analyzing Evidence for the Long Essay Question (LEQ)

Directions: For this set of exercises, you will practice all the skills covered so far in this book:

Step 1: Identify the tasks and terms

Step 2: Brainstorm specific evidence

Step 3: Develop a thesis and categories of evidence, and then outline your argument

Step 4: Write an opening paragraph.

Then, using your outline as a guide, write three body paragraphs, remembering that each time you introduce new evidence, you must also explicitly state why it matters to your thesis. Don't worry about writing style, transitions, or the closing—those things will be covered later in the book. Additionally, don't worry about timing and pacing. For now, it is more important to focus all of your attention on developing a written response that meets all the requirements of the AP LEQ rubric.

> **Exercise Question:** In what ways and for what reasons did the roles of women change in China during the Tang Dynasty?

Explanation

Although you may have used different evidence and an entirely unique argument, look at the following explanation and check that you completed each step.

Tasks: In what ways AND for what reasons

Terms: roles of women, change, China, Tang Dynasty

Categories of Evidence:

Early Tang emperors, ruling in a time of peace, loosened restrictions on women

Wu Zetian enacted policies that directly or indirectly benefitted women

Later Tang rulers, in less peaceful times, reverted to more restrictive policies

Sample Thesis: Early Tang rulers, free of the threat of invasion or rebellion, loosened social restrictions on women in China and created an environment that allowed for the ascension of Wu Zetian to the throne, which resulted in even less restrictive policies under her rule, however, Tang rulers who followed Wu gradually reverted to more restrictive policies, partly because of the changing political environment and partly in response to Wu herself.

Sample Body Paragraph: Wu Zetian enacted policies which, directly or indirectly, benefitted women. She emphasized the value of education by improving on the system created by her predecessors and inviting scholars to replace military figures as her court advisors. These education policies encouraged more families to educate their daughters as well as their sons. Wu also elevated the importance of education by relying more heavily on merit in the selection of government officials. By expanding the Civil Service System, she attracted the most qualified people in China to official positions. Even Chinese peasants, who might not have had access to the education available to the nobility, benefitted from Wu's policies. As emperor, Wu helped to lower taxes on peasants and provide them with more land for farming, thus improving peasant life while simultaneously increasing China's agricultural production.

Review your response to the preceding exercise. The evidence that you provided was based upon information that you could recall from your previous work in World History. Did your evidence include any of the details in the sample above? You might want to check the list of Key Terms in the Appendix to see if there are other relevant details that could have been used with your argument.

Taking the Next Step

You've successfully written the body of an LEQ. The technique you used for evidence analysis in the LEQ works equally well in any thesis essay, so your hard work here will help you in college as well as on the AP exam. Now get ready, because next we will apply those new skills to body paragraphs in the DBQ.

In-body Document Analysis and Citation for the DBQ

The title of this section is long! However, to be totally descriptive, it would have to read "DBQ Document In-body Evidence and Critical Analysis and Methods of In-body Document Citation"—but that would be ridiculous. Basically, this section applies the skills you have just practiced in the previous section to DBQ essays.

For the DBQ, you will introduce and analyze documents included with the question, in addition to specific evidence that you can recall from your own study of World History. Just as with the LEQ, each time you introduce a new document or piece of specific evidence, you must explicitly state why it matters to your thesis. You will also include analysis of the document source at this time (see Step 2). Finally, each document should be cited within the body of your essay. If you have analyzed the source for a particular document, you will have already included a citation within the body of your essay. If not, you should still credit the source as it is noted in the document. Although explicit citation is not required by the rubric, you are required to use documents explicitly and individually, and citation is evidence of that use. In addition, when you write essays in your undergraduate classes, contextual citations demonstrate a mastery of the evidence and a sophistication of argument.

Here are a few examples of citations that might be found within successful DBQ essays citing the following document:

Document G

> SOURCE: **Sun Tzu, Chinese military theorist, from *The Art of War*, circa 5th c. BCE**
>
> There is no instance of a country having benefited from prolonged warfare. It is only one who is thoroughly acquainted with the evils of war who can thoroughly understand the profitable way of carrying it on.

"According to Sun Tzu, ..."

"As stated by Sun Tzu in the 5th century BCE, ..."

"Sun Tzu, a Chinese military theorist, stated..."

"Document G says..."

"...(Doc G)"

"...(Sun Tzu)"

"According to Sun Tzu, ... (Doc G)"

Even though there is no particular format that earns greater credit from the readers, I encourage my students to use something similar to the last example. The parenthetical citation is redundant in this example, but it is a worthwhile redundancy. The contextual citation ("According to Sun Tzu") is the most elegant way to note authorship in any kind of research assignment; however, it is not necessarily the most obvious at a glance. Although the AP Reader will spend several minutes reading your essay, and will definitely recognize a contextual citation as a valid reference to the document, if the reader, for any reason, finds it necessary to go back and quickly count the number of documents included in your essay, the parenthetical citation ("(Doc G)") is the most obvious. It only takes a moment longer to write, but it could mean the difference between a 7 and a 5.

While the most important part of any AP essay (LEQ or DBQ) is the thesis, 5 of the 7 possible points of the DBQ rubric are determined by the quality of your body paragraphs. To make certain that you score the points you need, always ask the following questions:

- Have you supported your thesis with six of the documents explicitly, individually, and correctly? **—2 points**
- Have you critically analyzed the source in at least three of the documents? **—1 point**
- Have you supported your thesis with at least one piece of specific evidence from outside the documents? **—1 point**
- Have you used your evidence to corroborate, qualify, or modify your argument? **—1 point**

Guided Practice: Analyzing Evidence for the DBQ

Directions: For the following exercise, follow the process outlined in the preceding steps.

Step 1: Identify the tasks and terms

Step 2: Read and analyze the documents and brainstorm outside evidence (make notes in the margins)

Step 3: Develop a thesis and categories of evidence, and then outline your argument (grouping documents and outside evidence within your categories)

Step 4: Write an opening paragraph.

Then, using your outline as a guide, write three body paragraphs, remembering that each time you introduce a new document or piece of specific evidence, you must explicitly state why it matters to your thesis. Critically analyze the source wherever you can, and, for each document, develop the habit of combining a contextual citation with a sentence-ending parenthetical citation.

Exercise Question: To what extent were the Mongols responsible for the resurgence of Silk Road trade in the 13th and 14th centuries?

Document A

SOURCE: **Marco Polo, Venetian traveler, from** *The Travels*, **Chapter XXVI, "HOW THE KAAN'S POSTS AND RUNNERS ARE SPED THROUGH MANY LANDS AND PROVINCES," circa 1300.**

Now you must know that from this city of Cambaluc [present-day Beijing] proceed many roads and highways leading to a variety of provinces, one to one province, another to another; and each road receives the name of the province to which it leads; and it is a very sensible plan. And the messengers of the Emperor in travelling from Cambaluc, … find at every twenty-five miles of the journey a station which they call *Yamb*, or, as we should say, the "Horse-Post-House." And at each of those stations used by the messengers, there is a large and handsome building for them to put up at, in which they find all the rooms furnished with fine beds and all other necessary articles in rich silk, and where they are provided with everything they can want. If even a king were to arrive at one of these, he would find himself well lodged.

Document B

> SOURCE: **Twitchett, Denis Crispin, John King Fairbank, and Albert Feuerwerker. From *The Cambridge History of China*, 1978.**
>
> The reputation of the *ortogh* in Yuan China is one of base collusion with the Mongolian overlords whose capital, wrung from the exploited Chinese population, was then lent to the *ortogh* to finance their, at best, shady operations that harmed government and people. The Mongols and Western Asians in high positions clearly did lend money to the *ortogh* merchants, who in turn lent it at usurious rates to units of local government that could not otherwise meet tax payments or to individuals facing similar financial needs, and then they relied on their special relation with the governors to collect their debts. The merchants' reputation for unbridled avarice may be exaggerated, but ordinary persons seem to have regarded them as the cause of much general suffering. Descriptive comments of the time often note that the Western Asian *ortogh* merchants "understood the ways of cities," where commerce was conducted, and ruthlessly used those skills to fatten their own purses and those of their Mongolian masters.

Document C

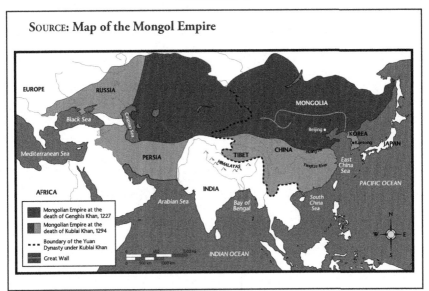

SOURCE: **Map of the Mongol Empire**

Document D

SOURCE: **Morris Rossabi, *Asian Topics in World History: The Mongols in World History*, from "Merchant Associations Alleviate the Perils of Caravan Trade," 2004.**

The Mongols recognized that the caravan trade across Eurasia was extraordinarily expensive for any single merchant. Often there would be as many as 70 to 100 men on each mission, and all had to be fed and paid and provided with supplies (including camels, horses, and so on) over a lengthy period of time.

Quite a number of the caravans simply did not make it, either because of natural disasters of one sort or another or plundering by bandit groups. Travelers, for example, mentioned coming across numerous skeletons, animal and human, on these routes. Because of the expense involved in such a disaster, just one such failed caravan could devastate an individual merchant's holdings.

The Mongol solution to these concerns was the establishment of *Ortogh*— through which merchants could pool their resources to support a single caravan. If a caravan did not make it, no single merchant would be put out of business. The losses would be shared, as would any risks, and of course, profits when the caravans succeeded. The Mongols also provided loans to merchants at relatively low rates of interest, as long as they belonged to an *Ortogh*.

Document E

SOURCE: **Silk Road: Dialogue, Diversity and Development, by the UNESCO Silk Roads Online Initiative.**

Found along the Silk Roads from Turkey to China, [caravanserais] provided not only a regular opportunity for merchants to eat well, rest and prepare themselves in safety for their onward journey, [but] also to exchange goods, trade with local markets and buy local products, and to meet other merchant travelers, and in doing so, to exchange cultures, languages and ideas.

As trade routes developed and became more lucrative, caravanserais became more of a necessity, and their construction intensified across Central Asia from the 10th century onwards, and continued until as late as the 19th century. This resulted in a network of caravanserais that stretched from China to the Indian subcontinent, Iran, the Caucasus, Turkey, and as far as North Africa, Russia and Eastern Europe, many of which still stand today.

Caravanserais were ideally positioned within a day's journey of each other, so as to prevent merchants (and more particularly, their precious cargos) from spending days or nights exposed to the dangers of the road. On average, this resulted in a caravanserai every 30 to 40 kilometers in well-maintained areas.

Document F

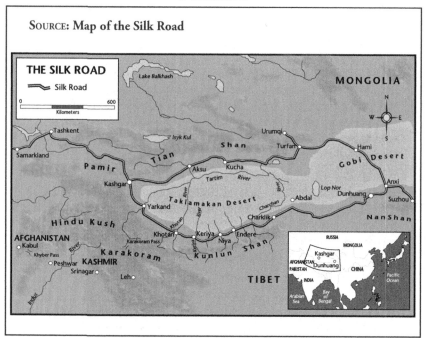

Source: **Map of the Silk Road**

Document G

SOURCE: *The Travels of Ch'ang Ch'un to the West, 1220-1223*, recorded by his disciple, Li Chi Ch'ang, translated by E. Bretschneider, 1888.

We were told, also, that the city of Sün-sz'-kan [Samarkand] lay more than 10,000 li [Chinese "mile" – approximately one-third of a US mile] to the southwest, that it was built on the best place in the country of the Hui-ho [Muslims], and that it was the capital of the K'i-tan dynasty, of which seven emperors had reigned there.

On the 13th of the sixth month, 1221, we passed over a mountain called Ch'ang sung ling [Mountain of High Pines], and stopped on the other side. There were so many pines and kuai trees. ...

On the 14th we passed over a mountain, crossed a shallow river, and passed the night in a plain. It was frightfully cold, and the next morning we found a thin coat of ice on the water. The natives said that generally in the fifth or sixth month snow begins to fall in this country, and that, happily, this year it was not so cold as in other years; therefore the master changed the name of the mountain into Ta hag ling [Mountain of the Great Cold]. Rain here is always accompanied by hail.

Thence we went more than a hundred li to the southwest, through a mountainous country, on a winding road. There was a stony river, more than fifty li long, the banks of which were about a hundred feet high. ... The mountains stretched to the west in a continuous chain, all covered with tall pine trees. We were five or six days travelling in these mountains, the road winding round the peaks.

Document H

> Source: Liu, Xinru. *The Silk Road in World History.* Oxford University Press, 2010.
>
> Genghis Khan was born during China's Song Dynasty (960-1279). At that time, China had a robust economy, with a large export sector supplying foreign demand. Silk yarn and silk textiles were still important exports, even though their availability outside China was increasing due to the spread of production techniques. Increased quantities of spices and incense, no longer used just for cooking and rituals, but now also for medicinal properties, were also being traded from the Arabian peninsula as well as Southeast and South Asia. Agricultural development had also led to population increases in Eurasia and Africa, thereby increasing the demand for local and imported commodities.
>
> In addition to China's traditional products, tea and porcelain drinking vessels associated with tea drinking, as well as porcelain dishes, enjoyed an international boom. Tea was especially popular among the nomads. Indeed, it was so popular that the tea-horse trade had replaced the old silk-horse trade on the northern borders of the Song Empire. Tea was also a favorite in Japan and the Islamic countries. Although porcelain ware was related to the tea culture, it was also independently significant. It, too, contributed to the growth in maritime trade, since its relative fragility meant that it had to be packed in bulky and heavy containers, and its transport by ships was much more efficient than by caravans. It was in large part due to the demand for porcelain that countries all along the coasts of the Indian Ocean and the western Pacific became involved in the maritime trade.

Explanation

Although you may have used different evidence and an entirely unique argument, look at the following explanation and check that you completed each step.

Tasks: To what extent (In what ways AND In what ways NOT)

Terms: Mongols, resurgence, Silk Road, trade, 13th and 14th centuries

Categories of Evidence:

Mongols conquered much of the Silk Road territory in the 13th century

Mongols created the Yam system for communication and transportation

Silk Road trade was driven by demand for foreign goods

Sample Thesis: To the extent that the Mongols conquered and secured much of the Silk Road, and created the Yam system to ease communication and transport across Asia, they helped spur a resurgence of trade along the route in the 13th and 14th centuries; however, to the extent that the western demand for Chinese products was high even before the birth of Genghis Khan, Mongol influence was only secondary.

Sample Body Paragraph: The Yam system, created to ease Mongol travel and communication across Asia, ultimately made Silk Road trade safer and easier in the 13th and 14th centuries. Ch'ang Ch'un described Silk Road travel in the early 13th century as long and strenuous. (Doc G) Since Ch'ang makes no mention of the Yams, it can be assumed they were not yet in place. By contrast, Marco Polo praises the utility of these way stations every 25–45 miles by the end of the 13th century. (Doc A) His trip across the Silk Road, using the Yams as stopovers, sounds much more enjoyable than did Ch'ang Ch'un's. Some of these Yams may have even served as the sites of future caravanserai which were also spaced at about 25–45 miles apart. (Doc E).

Review the body paragraphs that you wrote for the preceding exercise. Make certain that in each body paragraph, you have clearly demonstrated the relevance of your evidence in support of your thesis. As you have structured your thesis according to categories of evidence that respond to the terms of the essay question, so your paragraphs should move smoothly from one to the next, providing evidence that logically develops your thesis.

A Note About Historical Complexity

"It's complicated, Dad." I hear this almost every day when talking with my 15-year-old daughter, Mia.

"How was school today?" I ask, believing the answer to be pretty straightforward.

"It's complicated, Dad."

"Is everything ok with your friends?"

"It's complicated, Dad."

"What's up with your boyfriend?"

"It's complicated, Dad."

Are there no easy answers? As a matter of fact, in life, as in history, there actually are no easy answers. If you find an easy answer, it's likely that you misunderstood the question.

Historical complexity is simply the recognition that there are no easy answers. In any historical argument, there will be evidence that contradicts, evidence that corroborates, and evidence that qualifies the argument. Great essays account for and explain these contradictions, corroborations, and qualifications. Here's an example from the French Revolution:

> **The Point:** Women in the French Revolution achieved a high level of equality with men.
>
> ### Corroborating Evidence:
>
> • Condorcet argued for complete civil equality for women in 1789
>
> • Women joined the Cercle Social to discuss women's rights in 1790
>
> • Olympe de Gouges published *Declaration of the Rights of Woman* in 1791
>
> • Women formed the Society of Revolutionary Republican Women in 1793

- The French Republic referred to men and women as "citizens"

Qualifying Evidence:

- Women's clubs primarily focused on equality in marriage and education
- Most women participated in the revolution by supporting the efforts of their husbands
- The French words used for "citizen" are gender specific

Contradicting Evidence:

- Rousseau's writing, on which much of the revolution was based, specifically argued against women in the political sphere
- *The Declaration of the Rights of Man* and *Citizen*, a seminal work of the revolution, made no mention of women (a fact that motivated Olympe de Gouges to publish her declaration in 1790)
- Women's clubs were outlawed in 1793
- Olympe de Gouges was guillotined in 1793
- French women never gained the right to vote or hold office until 1944

It should be clear from this example that history is not black and white. Most historical arguments try to make sense of various shades of gray. That is the essence of historical complexity.

Taking the Next Step

Now that you've mastered each body paragraph, analyzing evidence and document sources, it's time to polish the spaces between your paragraphs with transition sentences. In the following section, you will learn how to provide effective transitions between your paragraphs and help your reader to follow the logic of your argument.

Transitions for Improved Analysis

Transitions make your essay sound better. Transitions help connect your ideas to each other. Transitions make your argument flow more smoothly. You should learn to use transitions. That's the point of this section of the book (without transitions).

Sounds a little choppy, right?

Now let's try to connect the ideas. Transitions make your essay sound better, but, more importantly, they help connect your ideas to each other. Since transition sentences can be used to explicitly connect the categories of evidence in your argument, they make your argument flow more smoothly. A smoother argument will sound much more persuasive, so you should learn to use transitions to improve the quality of your essays.

Better, right?

I'm sure your English teacher has given you a list of transition words that you should incorporate into your essays, such as "therefore," "however," "moreover," or "thus." At the root of this list is the idea that some words and phrases are very effective at joining separate-but-related, ideas. In a thesis essay, like the AP World History LEQ or DBQ, all the separate ideas are related to the thesis, so transitions are an appropriate means of connecting them. Although sometimes you will utilize your English teacher's list, more often, you will develop your transition sentences from the ideas themselves. The process is really very easy and, with practice, writing transitions will become second nature to you.

To create the best transitions, start with the logic of your argument. In Step 2, you practiced developing categories of evidence to support your thesis. In Step 3, you were encouraged to create analytical thesis statements by explicitly stating WHY or HOW your categories support your argument. Those WHYs and HOWs force you to assemble your categories of evidence in the most logical order to support your argument. Transition sentences simply reinforce this order. Look, for example, at the following question:

> **Example Question:** *Compare and contrast the influence of nationalism on the 20th century independence movement of Vietnam and the 19th century unification of Germany.*

An acceptable thesis might respond, "In both Vietnam and Germany, government officials, with their own agenda, were able to use a popular spirit of nationalism to accomplish their goals; German officials, however, were able to utilize their significant military advantage in Europe to minimize foreign influence on the process, whereas their Vietnamese counterparts had to contend with powerful outside forces, first French then American, as well as some resistance from within." Transition words in the thesis include *however* and *whereas*. These transitions are made possible by the order of our argument. Essentially, we're arguing that Germany and Vietnam were both assisted by nationalism, but in Germany the government used its significant military prowess to effectively minimize internal resistance and external interference while the nationalist movement in Vietnam was stymied for a time by a combination of internal resistance and external interference by a more powerful enemy.

If we move on to the body of this essay, we'll see how these explicit statements of logic within our thesis serve as the foundation for the transitions between each paragraph. According to the order we've established in this thesis, the first body paragraph should analyze evidence demonstrating the ways in which the German and Vietnamese governments utilized nationalism to further their goals. The second body paragraph will detail how and why German officials retained control of the nationalist movement, while the third body paragraph will analyze the evidence that demonstrates the Vietnamese government's lack of control over the same movement as a result of internal and external interference.

No matter what details you decide to include in these paragraphs, the transition between the first two body paragraphs could read, "Despite the similarities in outcomes for Germany and Vietnam, the process for each country was very different." We can reinforce these differences with a transition between the second and third body paragraphs that says, "Whereas Germany was able to minimize internal and external forces of resistance and control the nationalist spirit within its territories, Vietnamese officials had to contend with resistance from within and powerful interference from without while it attempted to steer its own nationalist movement." Essentially, these two sentences do the same thing as "however" and "whereas" in the opening paragraph.

I hope you can see that transition sentences, as used above, make the logic of your argument more explicit to the reader. Your essay may be good without them, but it will be fantastic with them. As you proceed through the rest of this book, try to develop the habit of adding a sentence at the end of each body paragraph that serves to explicitly connect your main ideas and make your argument flow more smoothly. You can begin developing that habit with the exercise that follows.

Guided Practice: Analytical Transitions

Directions: For the following exercise, you will continue to practice all the skills covered so far in this book:

Step 1: Identify the tasks and terms

Step 2: Brainstorm specific evidence (and analyze the documents in the DBQ)

Step 3: Develop a thesis and categories of evidence, and then outline your argument

Step 4: Write an opening paragraph

Step 5: Analyze your specific evidence in three body paragraphs

Now, using the example above as a model, write a transition sentence between the first and second body paragraph and another one between the second and third. Your transitions should connect the main ideas of your argument. Remember that transitions are not simply exercises in good writing style, but can reinforce the logic of your argument for the reader.

Exercise Question: *To what extent were the Mongols responsible for the resurgence of Silk Road trade in the 13th and 14th centuries?*

Explanation

Sample Thesis: To the extent that the Mongols conquered and secured much of the Silk Road, and created the Yam system to ease communication and transport across Asia, they helped spur a resurgence of trade along the route in the 13th and 14th centuries; however, to the extent that the western demand for Chinese products was high even before the birth of Genghis Khan, Mongol influence was only secondary.

Sample Transition: *(insert between the second and third body paragraphs)* While the Mongol conquest of the Silk Road region may have made travel safer and easier, the resurgence of trade across the Silk Road may be more closely linked to western demand for Chinese goods.

Taking the Next Step

At this point, you have mastered every part of the essay that earns points on the AP rubrics. But there is still one more piece of the puzzle—the closing paragraph. Although seemingly "pointless" (according to the rubrics), the final paragraph of your essay may hold the key to your ultimate success.

Step 5 Writing the Body

Sticking the Landing
—The Closing Paragraph

In 1996 the U.S. Women's Gymnastics Team won the gold medal, but the team's ultimate fate came down to the final competitor in the final event. As Team USA entered its final event, vaulting, the NBC commentators were giddy with excitement because the girls already had a commanding lead over the Russians and it certainly seemed like a lock. But then, the unthinkable happened. Jaycie Phelps started the event with an aerial feat so unique and spectacular that it bears her name—The Phelps. Every muscle in her 16-year-old legs flexed to power her down the runway toward the horse. She leapt into the air, propelled her body skyward off the horse, twisting and tumbling with such speed that it was nearly impossible to recount the entire routine. But, just as she spun into her blind landing, the forward momentum of her body as her feet hit the ground forced her to take a short hop before coming to a complete stop. The crowd gasped, and her parents dropped their heads into their hands in disbelief. That hop cost Jaycie and her team at least one-tenth of a point, and her final score of 9.662 opened a door for the Russian team to move up.

A series of similarly flawed vaults, including three falls in a row, left the fate of Team USA in the hands of young Kerri Strug. Under normal conditions, Kerri would be a good bet. But in this instance, because of the mistakes of her teammates, she needed an almost perfect 9.7 to win the gold for her team. Additionally, she had fallen on her first attempt, spraining her ankle and earning only a 9.162.

So now, after limping back to the start of the runway, Kerri Strug had to complete a one-and-a-half twist and land it with perfection on only one strong leg. At this point, the TV commentators were voicing the concerns of every distraught U.S. fan watching the event. Kerri gathered herself, raced down the runway—her ankle already throbbing—hit the horse and sprung into the air, and in an unbelievable demonstration of courage, Kerri Strug *stuck the landing*—picture perfect. The crowd erupted with excitement, and Team USA won the gold! The force of that landing damaged Kerri's ankle even further and, amid the applause, she fell to the ground and needed help to get back to her team. Kerri's score? 9.712—all because she stuck the landing!

Lasting Impressions

Fortunately, the AP essays are not much like Olympic gymnastics. If you do everything right in the opening and body of your essay, the closing paragraph doesn't really matter to your score. In fact, according to the rubrics, you don't even need a closing paragraph. So why even include this section in the book? Because your closing paragraph is, in fact, similar to Olympic gymnastics in one crucial way—the applause. As you've read earlier, the AP essays are not machine-scored. Real people read the essays and apply the AP standards to determine the scores. A strong closing paragraph restates your thesis, recounts your argument, and reminds the Reader about your best evidence and exactly why you deserve the top score!

The best part is that writing a great closing paragraph is way easier than sticking the landing at the end of the vault. In fact, you already did most of the heavy lifting when you wrote your opening paragraph. Just like the opening, your closing paragraph should include statements explaining the importance of each of your categories of evidence and a restatement of your thesis. Unlike your opening, the category statements within your closing paragraph should allude to the best evidence from the body of your essay.

So, what can you do to insure that your closing paragraph is more than just a dull restatement of your opening—a misstep on the landing? Begin with the reason you are writing the closing in the first place: the applause. You need to show your reader, in one final magnificent ta-da, that your argument is worth every bit of a 7 on the DBQ rubric (6 on the LEQ rubric). Review the logical steps of your argument one category at a time, and each time you state one of these generalizations, allude to that category's strongest piece of specific evidence for illustration. Then, after you've refreshed your categories of evidence, use the momentum of this powerful reformulation of your argument to clearly restate your thesis. All that will remain to be done is to catch your breath, stand up straight, raise your arms, and bask in the glory of victory.

Need further clarification? Let's look at an example.

Example Question: Describe and analyze the tactics used by Ho Chi Minh to gain independence for Vietnam between 1920 and 1969.

Here is one example of an opening paragraph:

Sample Opening Paragraph: As a child of political activists, Ho Chi Minh began his push for independence in the 1920s with his introduction to European communism. After Japan was expelled from Vietnam in WWII, he requested the assistance of the international community to support a nationalist independence movement. In the absence of international support, Ho Chi Minh embarked on the military struggle that would eventually lead to Vietnamese independence. The tactics used by Ho Chi Minh to gain independence for Vietnam seemed to escalate throughout the period 1920 to 1969 from philosophical revolution to military insurgence, however his desire to gain international support for the independence movement was consistent throughout the period.

Although you haven't been asked to write an entire essay, you might have envisioned some very good, specific evidence to follow this opening paragraph. For instance, your first body paragraph might have mentioned that Ho Chi Minh was introduced to Communism as a young man when he worked in London and Paris. You may have mentioned that he changed his name to "Nyugen the Patriot" and then to "He who has been enlightened" (Ho Chi Minh). As a communist leader, he helped form the French Communist Party, several communist youth organizations, the Viet Minh, and the National Liberation Front. Based on the structure of the sample thesis at the end of the opening paragraph above, your second paragraph would probably have continued with the formation of the Democratic Republic of Vietnam in 1945 and Ho Chi Minh's military struggles with the French and the Americans, including Dien Bien Phu and the Geneva Conference. Remaining parallel to the sample opening, your third body paragraph would have focused on Ho's continued attempts at international cooperation, beginning with his attempt to enlist the support of the Versailles Peace Conference in 1919 and the Paris Peace Conference in 1945, and continuing with the Geneva Agreement of 1954. To reinforce this final point, you might have included information about Ho Chi Minh's work to settle the differences between the Soviet Union and China.

The following closing paragraph will state each of these points and conclude with a slightly reformulated thesis.

> **Sample Closing Paragraph:** Ho Chi Minh began his push for Vietnamese independence as a communist activist, establishing himself as a party leader in France, the Soviet Union, and China. Eventually, his revolutionary thought led to violence when he launched his Viet Minh military campaign against the French and then the Americans. However, throughout his entire career, Ho Chi Minh attempted to enlist the support of the international community, beginning in 1920 when he petitioned the Versailles Peace Conference to support self-determination for the people of Vietnam. The tactics used by Ho Chi Minh to gain independence for Vietnam may appear to have escalated throughout the period 1920 to 1969 from mere participation in philosophical groups to the eventual violent military insurgence for which he is most famous, but closer examination reveals that Ho's ongoing attempts at international cooperation were a consistent foundation for his independence movement.

That's it. This paragraph summarizes the argument and drives home the thesis.

Here is one final note about closing paragraphs. **Never introduce new arguments at the end of the essay.** This is especially true for evaluative arguments—statements that preach a moral—but is equally true for statements attempting to earn Synthesis credit by expanding the argument. Although these closing statements will not hurt you on the rubric, remember that the closing paragraph is largely for effect. New arguments tend to distract the reader from the point you were attempting to drive home. Many well-meaning— but misguided—students may have ended the example paragraph above with, "It is time we reevaluate the Vietnam War in light of this evidence. The United States was the imperialist aggressor and Ho Chi Minh has been the historical scapegoat for too long." This final statement, suddenly attempting to assess the intentions of the United States in the Vietnam War, could be as damaging to the overall effect of the essay as a gymnast's belly-flop onto the mat.

Guided Practice: Effective Closing Paragraphs

Directions: For the following exercise, practice all the skills covered so far in this book.

Step 1: Identify the tasks and terms

Step 2: Analyze the documents and brainstorm specific evidence

Step 3: Develop a thesis and categories of evidence, and then outline your argument

Step 4: Write an opening paragraph

Step 5: Analyze your specific evidence in three body paragraphs and insert analytical transitions

Then, using the example shown above in this section ("Ho Chi Minh and Vietnamese Independence") as a guide, write a closing paragraph for your essay. Remember that this final paragraph is your best opportunity to "stick the landing" in your essay. Summarize each part of your argument, alluding to your most significant evidence, and restate your thesis—ta-da!

Exercise Question: *Analyze the connection between peace and financial success in Venice in the 15th and 16th centuries.*

Document A

Source: **Tommaso Mocenigo, Doge of Venice, on joining Florence in war against Milan, February 1422**

In our time, we have seen Giovanni-Galeazzo, Duke of Milan, who conquered all Lombardy, save Florence, the Romagna, and the Campagna di Roma, reduced to such straits by his expenses that he was obliged to remain quiet during five years; and it was with much ado then that he paid his troops. So it happens to all. If you preserve peace, you will amass so much money, that all the world will hold you in awe. My Lords, you see how, year by year, in consequence of the troubles of Italy, families migrate hither, and help to swell our population. If the Florentines give themselves to the Duke, so much the worse for them who interfere! Justice is with us. They have spent everything, and are in debt. We have a capital of 10,000,000, on which we gain 4,000,000. Live in peace, fear nothing, and trust not the Florentines! ... We wage battle against the Infidels only; and great are the praise and glory which we reap. So long as I live, my Lords, I will maintain those principles which I have hitherto followed, and which consist in living at peace!

Document B

Source: **Tommaso Mocenigo, Doge of Venice, on his deathbed, 1422**

Our City at present sends abroad for purposes of trade in various parts of the world 10,000,000 ducats a year, of which the interest is not less than 2,000,000. ... We find 1,000 gentlemen with means varying between 700 and 4,000 ducats a year. If you continue to prosper in this manner, you will become masters of all the gold in Christendom. But, I beseech you, keep your fingers from your neighbours, as you would keep them out of the fire, and engage in no unjust wars: for in such errors God will not support princes!

Document C

> SOURCE: **Pietro Orio, speaking against the election of Francesco Foscari as Doge, April 1423**
>
> ...if he was made Doge, Venice would be perpetually at war.

Document D

> SOURCE: **Francesco Foscari, Doge of Venice, speaking of war with Milan, December 3, 1425**
>
> Carmagnola's [Francesco Bussone, Count of Carmagnola] speech has laid before you the power and the resources of Filippo [Filippo Visconti of Milan]. They are not so great as rumour has represented them. Nor should we be justified in looking for any other than a happy and prosperous conclusion to our enterprise under Carmagnola as the captain of our arms. For he is versed in war; nor can all Italy show his equal this day in bravery and proficiency in the military art. Under such a general is offered us, beyond all doubt, the certain hope of extending our borders. All these considerations urge us to undertake the war with a good courage; a war, I repeat, which is necessary; for our enemy is powerful, neighbor to us, and aspires to the sovereignty of Italy. Let us embark upon this war, then, and avenge our wrongs by trampling in the dust our common foe, to the everlasting peace of Italy.

Document E

> SOURCE: **Giulio Porro, Venetian chronicler, on Milan's attack on the Venetian fleet, 1431**
>
> ...[Paolo Correr] on hearing the guns and seeing the ducal galleons bearing down, told Carmagnola that he ought either to attack Cremona (by way of causing a diversion) or to march down to the banks of the Po to support the doge's fleet, which had come up the river on his orders... .

Document F

SOURCE: **Philippe de Comines, French ambassador to Venice, 1495**

[Venice is] the most triumphant city that I have ever seen. ...impossible to describe the beauty, magnificence, and wealth. ...[the Grand Canal is] the most beautiful street in the world.

Document G

SOURCE: **Marin Sanudo, Venetian patrician, in an essay on the origins of Venice, 1493**

The city is about 7 miles in circumference; it has no surrounding walls, no gates which are locked at night, no sentry keeping watch as other cities have for fear of enemies; it is so very safe at present, that no one can attack or frighten it. As another writer said, its name has achieved such dignity and renown that it is fair to say Venice merits the title "Pillar of Italy," "deservedly it may be called the bosom of all Christendom."

Explanation

Sample Thesis: In Venice of the 15th and 16th centuries, peace was associated with economic prosperity, while war was generally associated with economic instability, except when the war was viewed as justified.

Sample Closing Paragraph: The Venetian view of peace and war is best exemplified by the words of the doge Tommaso Mocenigo who warned his people to, "engage in no unjust wars." The economic success of Venice had been built on her ability to stay out of the fray, and engage in commerce with all parties. Venetians would enter into war only with a just cause, like the defense of Christianity. They were so devoted to peace that Francesco Foscari, appealing for war with Milan, said that it would bring "everlasting peace to Italy." Throughout the 15th and 16th centuries, Venetians saw peace as the path to economic prosperity and war as the way to economic instability, except when the war was justified.

Taking the Next Step

Ta-da! You have stuck the landing! Review your conclusions and note how they flow organically from the logic of your paper. Pay attention to any techniques you used to move your readers smoothly out of your essay, without raising new issues or topics.

By now, you have learned—and hopefully mastered—the process of writing LEQ and DBQ essays. Note how writing a conclusion fits into that process. Now it is time to think about how you can accomplish that process within the time frame provided for the exam.

Preparing for the Exam

Beating the Clock

In my class, I spend most of the year trying to convince students to stop worrying about how long it takes them to answer the essay questions. "Focus on perfecting the process" is what I say; "worry about time and pacing later." Of course, on that one day in May, time matters, so you have to worry about it at some point. The problem with obsessing about time too soon is that it leads to bad habits. Writers who are worried about time omit some of their prewriting and often do a too-hasty job of brainstorming evidence. They erroneously believe that the solution to the time problem is writing from the moment the test booklet lands on the desk. This approach completely ignores everything we've discussed and practiced on the last 80+ pages. Remember, the rubrics reward good planning.

The real answer to improving your time on the essays is writing more essays. If you play a musical instrument, you likely learned to play the notes slowly. Speed came naturally as your skill improved. That's exactly what needs to happen with your essays. Master the steps of the writing process slowly at first, and then practice until your speed improves. *Mastering the Essay* provides plenty of practice for both LEQ and DBQ essays. In fact, if you have worked through each and every section, completing the practice exercises along the way, you are probably wondering why this section even exists. The practice exams in the Exercise Workbook are included to provide you with an opportunity (actually, three opportunities) to simulate the actual AP World History exam conditions. Each exercise requires that you write two essays (a DBQ and an LEQ), under the same time constraints imposed on the May exam. Furthermore, each of your LEQs must be chosen from among three questions, just like on the actual exam. Although this process may seem inconsequential, for some students the choice poses a significant barrier to their success.

Choosing an LEQ

There are many philosophies regarding the choice of an LEQ question, and many teachers will share their own theories with their students. Ultimately, there is no technique that is necessarily better than the rest. However, no matter what your method of decision-making, a few key points should be considered.

1. You must feel relatively comfortable with the terms of the question.

2. You must completely understand the tasks demanded in the question.

3. You must choose quickly, because the rubric offers no reward for your decision.

4. Each question will be assessed according to the same general standards, so there is no inherently better question.

5. Be very wary of a question that seems much easier than the others. Students often misread the tasks, which can lead to a partially off-topic response.

In the end, your choice must depend more on your understanding of history than on some strategy to outsmart the test-makers. As soon as you have finished writing your DBQ, move to the LEQ group, carefully read each question, quickly choose the one you would like to answer, and begin your pre-writing process. The choice should take you no more than a minute or two.

The test-makers recommend that you devote 45 minutes (after the 15-minute reading period) to the DBQ and 40 minutes to the LEQ. This is a good rule of thumb and, although the times are not required, you should make every attempt to follow these guidelines. As stated earlier in the book, it is quite normal for students to use more than 15 minutes for the DBQ prewriting, but since prewriting actually helps to shorten your writing time, you should still aim to finish writing the DBQ by the end of the first hour of the essay section of the exam.

You should never find yourself approaching the final essay with fewer than 20 minutes remaining. But, what if something extraordinary happens—sudden illness, loss of memory, asteroid falls to Earth—and you run out of time in the middle of writing your final essay? In this very unlikely event, you should write as much as you can until the final minute of the testing period. Then list all of your remaining evidence (from your brainstorming notes—never omit the prewriting steps) so the reader will be able to see that you knew what should have been included. If you have already written enough to demonstrate a good grasp of the tasks and terms of the question, this list might help. Of course, if you have followed all the steps recommended in this book, and you have completed all of the exercises, you will not need this last piece of advice.

Use the practice exams to develop a sense of good pacing. A great practice technique is to use a stopwatch to time each portion of the test. After you finish a practice test, review the times you spent on each of the essays and, if necessary, adjust your pacing on the next test. By the time you have completed all three practice tests, you will feel very confident about your performance on the upcoming AP World History exam.

Part 3

The Other Question Types

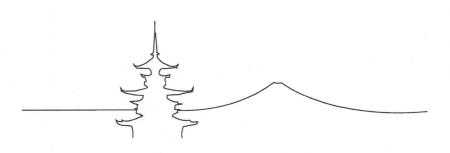

The New AP Multiple-Choice

Every September for 33 years, I've entered my classroom for the first time... again. And for most of those years, the classes I anticipated the most were the AP History courses. I love the stories of European and World history. I love the spirit of high school students willing to take on the challenge of an AP class. I love the personal challenge of trying to guide those students through a complicated chronology coupled with college-level writing skills until they can achieve the ultimate goal—a 5 on the AP exam.

You know what I don't love? The one question that is asked every year, and every year it grates on my nerves:

> "What's a good AP prep book?"

By "good," they mean chock full of little factoids they can cram to prepare for the Multiple-Choice section of the exam.

For years, I've responded with my standard, "They all stink! If you want history content, read the textbook and stay awake in class. If you want to do well on the AP exam, learn to write like a college freshman, because writing is what matters most on the AP exam." And every year, my students give me a polite nod and then go out and buy one, two, and sometimes three AP prep books.

So why am I so against the run-of-the-mill prep book? Because it is basically an outline of World history, thrown together by some big-box publisher who preys on the deepest fear expressed by most AP World History students—that they don't know or haven't memorized enough details for the MC section of the exam.

The reality is that nobody knows enough. **Most of the smartest kids in the country barely get half of the multiple-choice questions correct.**[1] So how do they get those 4s and 5s? Writing. Great essays add up to great scores.

But...

Since you will spend almost an hour answering multiple-choice questions on the exam, you might as well do the best you can. So let's take a look at the multiple-choice question format.

The New Format

On the AP exam, multiple-choice questions appear in sets of 2-5 questions based on a single document prompt. The document prompts might be excerpts from primary sources or secondary sources, charts, graphs, maps, or images.

The questions are designed in a way that makes them difficult (if not impossible) to answer with only the document, and equally difficult to answer with only your knowledge of history. **The questions require you to combine your analysis of the document with your understanding of history.**

Here's an example:

Questions 1–3 refer to the passage below.

> "Wretched Romans [citizens of Constantinople], how you have been led astray! You have departed from hope, which rests in God, by trusting in the power of the Franks [Western Europeans]. As well as the City itself, which will soon be destroyed, you have lost the true religion... Be aware, miserable citizens, what you are doing today... you have denied the true faith handed down to you by your forefathers. You have confessed your impiety. Woe to you when you are judged!"

> *Gennadios (formerly Georgios Scholarios), Byzantine monk, in a manifesto against union with the Western Church, November 1, 1452*

1. The passage illustrates the tensions generated by which of the following historical events?

   A. The Great Schism between the Eastern and Western Christians

   B. The impending threat of an Ottoman assault on Constantinople

   C. The posting of Martin Luther's 95 Theses

   D. The Venetian attack on Constantinople in the Fourth Crusade

2. Which of the following was most directly caused by the crisis associated with the passage?

   A. The fall of the Fatimid caliphate

   B. The Black Death

   C. The Italian Renaissance

   D. The First World War

3. Gennadios' criticisms are most similar to those of which of the following?

   A. Charles de Gaulle and his followers upon the surrender of France in 1940

   B. Martin Luther at the Diet of Worms

   C. Muhammed at Mecca in 632

   D. The defenders of Verdun in the First World War

As you can see, these ain't your father's multiple-choice questions! However, they do share several characteristics with previous multiple-choice questions from way back when. Most important among those characteristics is that you need not generate an answer from out of the blue—the correct response is right in front of you. Also, like earlier multiple-choice questions, the wrong answers are

---

1 – http://research.collegeboard.org/programs/ap/data

often designed specifically to serve as distracters—that is, they have elements of truth that might seem to relate to the topic but do not specifically answer the question. The differences between these new MC questions and their predecessors, however, are striking.

As stated earlier, it is nearly impossible to answer the questions without BOTH analyzing the document in the prompt AND remembering specific details from history. In this way, the test-makers hope to evaluate your understanding of history, as well as your historical thinking skills. Also, you may have noticed that each question includes only four answer choices—no more choice E. Along with the fifth choice, the test-makers have also eliminated the wrong answer penalty, so **answering every question, no matter what, is your best tactic**.

So let's see how well you did with the example questions.

Analyzing the Document

First, you needed to analyze the document prompt. Remember the **3-Step Process**? It works for MC questions on the new exam.

❶ **Summarize:** *What does the document say?*

It says that the citizens of Constantinople have abandoned their trust in God and instead put their faith in the Westerners. It implies that this is a mistake that will cause the downfall of Constantinople and the damnation of its citizens.

❷ **Analyze:** *Why does it matter?*

The document highlights the tensions among the people of the Roman Empire (Byzantines) in the mid-15th century. Among these stresses are the differences they have with the Roman Catholic Church of the West and the survival of the city of Constantinople.

❸ **Criticize:** *How might the source have influenced the meaning of the document?*

As a Byzantine monk, Gennadios is likely a strict adherent to the beliefs of the Eastern Orthodox Church, which by 1452, would be in stark contrast to those of the Roman Catholics. Consequently, his rabid attacks on the "Franks" (a pejorative term used to describe Western Europeans) might be a product of his own longstanding hatred of Roman Catholicism as much as any immediate crisis.

Next, it's time to answer the questions.

Analyzing the Answer Choices

Q1 - Contextualization

Question 1 is the easiest of the three because it simply requires an understanding of the basic historical context of the prompt. **Contextualization** is an important historical thinking skill, and one that will be assessed again and again on the new AP World History MC section. In this case, the relevant information is that Gennadios is worried about the well-being of the Byzantines and the document was written in 1452.

You should remember from your history class that the city of Constantinople fell to the Ottomans in 1453, so it could be that the stress in Gennadios' language is inspired by the threat of the Ottoman attack on the city—answer choice B. Notice that incorrect answers A and C allude to religious conflicts, which may seem connected to Gennadios' discussion of faith, but neither of which answers the question. Answer choice D is interesting because it discusses an event that preceded the document by 300 years, but with which you might be unfamiliar. It's an old-school MC question trick—"I don't know the answer to this question AND I don't know what this answer says, so, therefore, this answer must be correct." Not so. Don't fall for it.

Q2 - Causation

Causation is another important historical thinking skill that will be assessed many times in the multiple-choice section of the exam. Question 2 asks you to connect the crisis (the Fall of Constantinople) with some future effect of that crisis. Historians list several effects of the Ottoman conquest of Constantinople, and among them is the acceleration of the Italian Renaissance caused by the rapid influx of ancient Greek and Roman writings brought to Italy by Byzantine scholars escaping the Ottoman onslaught.

These "new" ideas helped to fuel an already smoldering humanism in Italy—answer choice C. Like in Q1, answer choice A harkens to the religious nature of the document. Answer D is somewhat more insidious because, if you know the connection at all, you might associate the rise of the Ottomans in 1453 with the fall of the Ottomans in WWI. The two are loosely connected but not necessarily cause-and-effect, and certainly not as directly causal as Constantinople and the Renaissance. Finally, choice B is another left-field response—it has no connection and is there simply to distract students who have little or no memory of the events of 1453.

Q3 - Comparison

Comparison, especially across time, is also assessed on the new MC section of the AP exam. Question 3 requires you to distill the essence of Gennadios' argument and to compare that with the argument of another historical actor in another historical period. Essentially, Gennadios is saying that the Byzantines have abandoned their own principles in favor of an antithetical position because they wish to save themselves in the moment. It is clear from the document that he believes they have now lost both their principles and their city. This sounds very much like the argument made by Charles de Gaulle and the Free French after Marshal Petain surrendered to the Nazis in 1940. De Gaulle and his followers believed that the Vichy government had sacrificed its principles for a false peace with Hitler—answer choice A. Answers B and C both conjure the religious nature of the document and answer choice D is another choice from out of the blue.

Short-Answer Questions

If you've ever seen the movie *Stand by Me*, you may remember the scene when Gordie ponders, "Mickey's a mouse, Donald's a duck, Pluto's a dog. What's Goofy?" This random question leaves the four best friends baffled as they try, but fail, to reason out the Disney character's true species.

Little did they know that even Art Babbitt, the Disney animator who created Goofy, had trouble defining the character. "Think of the Goof as a composite of an everlasting optimist, a gullible Good Samaritan, a half-wit..." wrote Babbitt in 1934. He conceded "a vague similarity" between Goofy and Pluto, but insisted that their animation made them "entirely different... One is dog. The other human." So what is Goofy?

Now, the Disney Corporation declares him to be a dog, but I'm not entirely sure that will settle the issue. After all, Disney's other dog, Pluto, wears only a collar, walks on all fours and even barks—he is definitely a dog. By contrast, Goofy is always featured in pants and a shirt, he always walks completely upright, and speaks in English—he never barks. Furthermore, he clearly has hands and feet—no paws. Disney may want to redefine Goofy, but if you wear your underwear on your head, can you really call it a hat?

The Hybrid Question

This is the issue with the newest member of the AP World History exam—the Short-Answer Question (SAQ). The College Board® has declared this to be a hybrid question format. It is neither a writing question nor strictly an objective question. Like the new Multiple-Choice Questions, the SAQs often begin with a document prompt, but then students are required to generate their own answers without any given choices. Sounds like a short essay, but the scoring criteria make the two open-ended question types "entirely different."

According to the College Board®, students need not formulate paragraphs or thesis statements in their responses. Bulleted answers are encouraged. So, the SAQ is neither essay nor MC; it is, in fact, an entirely new breed of AP question, and one you will need to be prepared to tackle.

Since you must generate your responses from scratch, thinking of the SAQ as a writing exercise can be most useful. You may not need to respond with a thesis, but as I am fond of saying in class, everything is a thesis. So treating this as a thesis exercise will not hurt you. The SAQ rubric requires you to make explicit connections within your answer, which sounds like analysis. So our approach will resemble that of the LEQ without the stress of worrying about form and style. Let's take a look at a couple of examples.

1. Use the document below and your knowledge of world history to answer all parts of the question that follows.

...Arthur T. Hadley said recently that those for whom the use of the A-bomb was "wrong" seem to be implying "that it would have been better to allow thousands on thousands of American and Japanese infantrymen to die in honest hand-to-hand combat on the beaches than to drop those two bombs." People holding such views, he notes, "do not come from the ranks of society that produce infantrymen or pilots." And there's an eloquence problem: most of those with firsthand experience of the war at its worst were not elaborately educated people. ...That is, few of those destined to be blown to pieces if the main Japanese islands had been invaded went on to become our most effective men of letters or impressive ethical theorists or professors of contemporary history or of international law.

On the other hand, John Kenneth Galbraith is persuaded that the Japanese would have surrendered surely by November without an invasion. He thinks the A-bombs were unnecessary and unjustified because the war was ending anyway. The A-bombs meant, he says, "a difference, at most, of two or three weeks." But at the time, with no indication that surrender was on the way, the kamikazes were sinking American vessels, the Indianapolis was sunk (880 men killed), and Allied casualties were running to over 7,000 per week. "Two or three weeks," says Galbraith. Two weeks more means 14,000 more killed and wounded, three weeks more, 21,000. Those weeks mean the world if you're one of those thousands or related to one of them. ...He worked in the Office of Price Administration in Washington.

In general, the principle is, the farther from the scene of horror the easier the talk. ...Winston Churchill, with an irony perhaps too broad and easy, noted in Parliament that the people who preferred invasion to A-bombing seemed to have "no intention of proceeding to the Japanese front themselves."

> *Paul Fussell, American literary scholar and US Army combat officer in WWII Europe, from "Thank God for the Atom Bomb," an article in* The New Republic, *August 1981.*

A. Provide ONE piece of evidence from outside of the document that weakens Hadley's argument about the connection between social class and opinions about the atomic bomb.

B. Provide ONE piece of evidence from outside of the document that weakens Galbraith's argument about the "necessity" of the bomb.

C. Provide ONE piece of evidence from another historical event that supports Fussel's argument about the connection between experience and opinion in general.

Like all SAQs, Question 1 is divided into three parts, all based on the original prompt. In this case, the prompt is a secondary source document. The prompt may be a primary or secondary source document, map, chart, graph, or image—or it might include no document at all. In Question 1 you are asked to read the document and provide evidence—first to weaken the two internal arguments, then to support the author's overall argument. Since this SAQ is based on a document, let's begin with document analysis.

Analyzing the Document

Once again, the 3-Step Process:

❶ **Summarize:** *What does the document say?*

The author argues that the debate over the ethics of the bombings of Hiroshima and Nagasaki is divided between those with firsthand war experience and those without. He cites two famous scholars and statistical evidence of the death toll in the Pacific as evidence to support his contention.

❷ **Analyze:** *Why does it matter?*

As a high school student, you may have been exposed to the opinions of many historians regarding the use of atomic weapons on Japan. The author has suggested a connection between the personal experience of a writer and the opinion expressed within his/her writing. This argument can provide context for other documents addressing the Hiroshima debate.

❸ **Criticize:** *How might the source have influenced the meaning of the document?*

Paul Fussel was a WWII veteran, so his personal experiences likely impacted his views on war. Even if we don't know specifically what he witnessed in the war, we can assume that he saw firsthand much of the brutality associated with the European theater. Additionally, he was a "literary scholar," which implies that he writes for a living and is likely quite skilled at developing strong written arguments. It should also be noted that the piece from which this excerpt has been drawn was an article in *The New Republic*, a generally liberal publication. All of this suggests that the author may have generally liberal political views that conflict with his more conservative opinion of the atomic bomb.

Explanation

So now onto the answers.

Part A asks for evidence that might weaken Hadley's contention that those who were most likely to engage in a ground war in 1945 Japan were less likely to become academics. One bit of evidence that you might remember from U.S. History is the GI Bill. The Serviceman's Readjustment Act of 1944 granted tuition and expenses for college to nearly half of the 16 million veterans returning from WWII. At that moment in history, only 5% of Americans had a college education, so by 1956, when the first GI Bill expired, WWII vets were 10 times more likely to be college educated than those with no war experiences. In fact, an acceptable response to this question might also cite any number of firsthand chronicles of war from World History – Thucydides (Peloponnesian Wars), Charles Francois (Napoleonic Wars), Erich Maria Remarque (WWI), and hundreds of others.

Part B requires evidence to weaken the argument made by Galbraith that the atomic bomb was unnecessary because the war would have ended in 2-3 weeks even with a ground invasion of Japan. Although his estimate may be defensible given the evidence available to us more than 70 years after the fact, consider the facts as they presented themselves in August 1945. Consider the Allied experience fighting Japan to that point. When U.S. Marines first landed at Tarawa, they were told to expect very little resistance on the little islet of Betio—a strip of land 3 miles long by half-mile wide. It took 76 hours and 3,000 US casualties to take the islet, and Betio was just the first of the Tarawa Islands. This experience supports two important arguments against Galbraith's contention—defeating the Japanese in battle was not easy or quick, and Allied commanders tended to underestimate the Japanese resistance.

Another bit of evidence that could be used against Galbraith is the Allied supply chain that had been assembled in preparation for the Japanese invasion forces. Despite their tendencies toward underestimation of Japan's forces, the Allied commanders had put in place logistics to supply and reinforce an invasion force until November 1946. So the commanders were prepared for over one year of ground fighting.

Finally, **Part C** asks for evidence to support Fussel's argument that authors without firsthand experience of an historical event are more likely to glorify or understate the ugly reality. Since the question specifically asks for "evidence from another historical event," you will want to cite examples from outside the context of WWII. There are plenty of examples of "glorious war" written by authors with no battlefield experience, and any one of them would be acceptable here. Many Islamic chroniclers, for instance, were employed by the Sultan to recount great events. These authors often did their work within the palace walls, limited to only the oral stories of others who had participated. Since the resulting "histories" would have had to have been approved by the Sultan, the writers would have been wise to insure that the stories made the empire look good.

Now that you understand the basic approach, here is another example of an SAQ. This one has a map. Check it out.

2. Use the map below and your knowledge of world history to answer all parts of the question that follows.

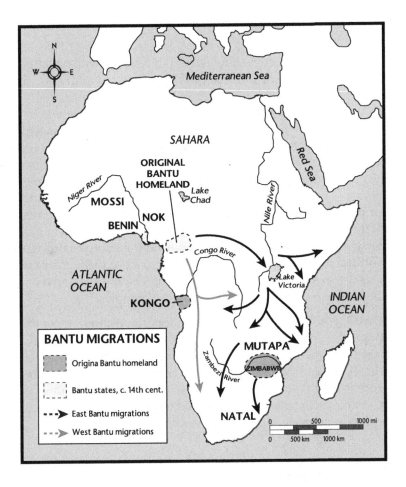

A. Identify and explain TWO agricultural factors that can help to explain the Bantu migrations as illustrated on the map.

B. Identify and explain ONE non-agricultural factor that can help to explain the Bantu migrations as illustrated on the map.

Explanation

Question 2 is a visual document—a map. You are asked to analyze the document and provide evidence—first to connect the map with agriculture, then to connect the map with something besides agriculture.

Part A can be answered in a few ways, but here we will explain ONE factor that may have contributed to WHY the Bantu migrated, and ONE factor that might help to explain WHERE they migrated. The first is the easiest, because it is a pattern repeated everywhere in world history. The Bantu people of western Africa were among the first African groups to develop farming. As they increased their food production, they also increased their capacity for population growth. About 3000 years ago, the Bantu experienced a population explosion and this was one reason why they migrated out from their homeland. As for where they migrated, the map shows that they moved east and south through largely arable lands that were previously occupied by hunter-gatherers. These new lands allowed the Bantu to utilize their agricultural technology and know-how, and since these places were homes only to small bands of hunter-gatherers, it was relatively easy for the Bantu to displace or absorb the local peoples.

For **Part B**, you might want to mention the iron technology of the Bantu people. Although the Bantu utilized iron for agricultural purposes, their iron-making skills became so exceptional that they developed a vast trade network based on iron products. That trade network is another explanation for the Bantu migration shown on the map. As more distant markets opened to the iron trade and demand grew, Bantu peoples migrated to meet the new demand.

Taking the Next Step

Although you still can't call the underwear on your head a hat and Goofy is still not exactly a dog, you might now begin to think of the Short-Answer Questions on the AP World History exam as writing exercises. You can probably see, from the two examples above, the ways in which you can apply your writing skills to earn full credit on the SAQ rubric. Fortunately for you, the Exercise Workbook for *Mastering the Essay* includes a full set of SAQ practice exercises. So practice away!

Appendix

Key Terms

The AP World History exam covers over 5,000 years of events, movements, concepts, and people from every corner of the earth. To suggest that I might list below the most important of these would be both arrogant and disingenuous. No one can adequately capture the essence of World History within a list of terms.

With this in mind, I humbly submit the following list as merely a springboard into the greater depths of World History. If you truly wish to review the content your teacher spent all year developing, I suggest that you begin with the AP World History Course and Exam Description published each year by The College Board®. It is updated each year with any changes in the exam or course structure, and it includes an excellent course framework that approaches the content from several perspectives. The list below begins with the six Historical Periods listed within the most recent of these publications, and proceeds with some key concepts to assist you in remembering content to support your essays. This list is neither necessary nor sufficient for a thorough understanding of World History, but I hope it is sufficient to jog your memory, encourage further research, and support your writing development. Good luck and write on!

Period 1: Beginnings to 600 BCE

Caste

Code of Ur-Nammu

Crop diffusion

Cuneiform

Egypt

Environmental impact

Foraging

Hammurabi's Code

Hieroglyphs

Hinduism

Hittites

Indus Valley

Iron tools and weapons

Judaism

Meso/South America

Mesopotamia

Monumental architecture

Neolithic revolution

Nile River

Pastoralism

Patriarchy

Pictographs

Plant and animal domestication

Polytheism

Population growth

Pyramids

Shamanism

Shang China

Social classes

Specialization of labor

Tigris and Euphrates Rivers

Trade and transportation

Water control

Yellow River

Ziggurats

Zoroastrianism

Period 2: 600 BCE to 600 CE

Buddhism

Christianity

City-states

Confucianism

Daoism

Disease

Greco-Roman

Greece and Rome

Gupta Empire

Huns

Migration

Monasticism

Xiongnu

Zhou and Han China

Period 3:   600 CE to 1450 CE

Aztec Empire

Banking

Bantu migration

Bedouins

Black Death

Caravans

China

Coinage

Crop diffusion

Dar al-Islam

Diaspora

Europe

Feudalism

Inca Empire

Islam

Khanates

Long distance trade

Maya civilization

Mongols

Neoconfucianism

Paper money

Polynesian migration

Tang and Song empires

Urban decline

Vikings

Period 4:   1450 CE to 1750 CE

Atlantic system

Atlantic World

Cartography

Colombian exchange

Decline of nomadic groups

European preeminence

Globalization

Gunpowder empires

Imperialism

Joint-stock companies

Literacy

Little ice age

Mercantilism

Mita and *encomienda*

Navigation

Plantation crops

Sea-based trade

Slave trade

Taxation

Key Terms

Period 5: 1750 CE to 1900 CE

Abolition

Capitalism

Enlightenment philosophies

Gender inequities

Global migration

Industrial revolution

Industrial world imbalance

Marxism

Meiji Japan

Middle class

Nationalism

Ottoman Empire

Private property

Qing Empire

Revolution and independence

Social Darwinism

Suffrage

The West

Transnational ideologies

Transoceanic empires

Urbanization and environment

Wealth imbalance

Working class

Period 6: 1900 CE to Present

Authoritarianism

Capitalism

Chinese Revolution

Cold War

Communism

Conflict and diplomacy

Decolonization

Deforestation

Democracy

Environmental impact

Family structures

Feminism

Gender roles

Global governance

Great Depression

Green Revolution

International Marxism

Land redistribution

Latin American Revolutions

Mass migrations

Medical innovations

Metropoles

Multinational corporations

Nationalism

New technology

Nonviolence

Oil and nuclear power

Peasant protest

Russian Revolution

Scientific innovations

Social reform and revolution

Socialism

Total war

A Letter to Teachers

THE PURPOSE OF THIS BOOK is to help you teach advanced historical thinking and writing skills to your AP World History students. I hope that its design facilitates that purpose and, in the process, makes your job a bit easier.

As a history teacher, you are responsible for teaching centuries of content as well as an ever-growing list of skills—among them writing. The balance between content and skill-development has always been challenging for teachers in our discipline, especially for Advanced Placement teachers, and the newest AP World exam format has made our job even more complicated. We know that our students cannot face the new AP exam in May without a thorough understanding of historical concepts, nor can they succeed on the exam without practicing skills of analysis and written expression. This book was originally written to provide you with a resource for helping your students to hone their writing skills within the context of the AP World course content, and that mission is even more urgent since the College Board® has redesigned the exam.

Mastering the Essay guides students through a process for developing consistently strong thesis essays—the kind of writing necessary for the AP LEQ and DBQ, as well as most college-level essays. The process is simple and straightforward, and each unit of this book focuses on a key step in that process. The exercises accompanying each step are arranged chronologically within the Exercise Workbook so that you can quickly and easily address any step of the process at any point throughout the year.

Beyond this book, Sherpa Learning is providing *Mastering the Essay* users with a variety of additional online resources, offering flexibility to pick and choose content and to continually access new resources. Online you will find sample essays, scoring guidelines for each exercise, instructional resources for use in and out of the classroom, writing skills lessons that can be easily adapted to fit any historical unit, and an online forum for you to collaborate with other AP World teachers. Additionally, since Sherpa Learning believes educational publishing is a dynamic process, new resources are constantly being added, therefore users have access to a constant influx of new materials.

I hope that *Mastering the Essay* will become an integral part of your AP World History instructional plans, and that you and your students benefit from the skill lessons and practice exercises in this book. It has always been my goal to create a resource that works within today's classroom. If you should have comments or suggestions that might help to further this goal, please contact me directly at Tony@MasteringTheEssay.com.

Tony Maccarella
January 2018

Author's Acknowledgments

M ASTERING THE ESSAY is the product of over 15 years of experience in the AP community. My many friends and colleagues at the annual AP Reading were indispensible in the creation and refinement of the *MTE* writing process. Although there are too many people to list them all, I would like to mention a few of the AP rock stars who had a direct hand in the development and success of this volume.

For their consistent encouragement about the book, teaching, and life in general, I am indebted to Carl Ackerman, Theresa Jesperson, Catherine Holden, Sharon Parker, and Bob O'Donnell. My good friends and former colleagues at Parsippany Hills, Steve Bechtler, Keith Campbell, and Robert Weinstein, were essential to the success of the First Edition and continued to "keep me in the game" as I worked through these revisions. Additionally, Kevin McCaffrey, Larry Treadwell, Matt Gutt, Jessica George, and Jerry Hurd, even after all these years, continue to spread the word about the value of the *MTE* writing process. I cannot thank them enough!

As I worked out the kinks in this newest revision, I was aided by my new friends and colleagues at Saddle River Day School. The SRDS family, including my AP World History students, provided me the opportunity to explore new ideas and continue with the professional development activities essential to remaining excited after 35 years in the business.

As in the past, I remain indebted to my publishers and friends, David Nazarian and Christine DeFranco at Sherpa Learning. Through their vision for Sherpa, David and Christine have helped me to create content of consistently high quality—a source of great pride.

Finally, again, I thank my family for their love and support. My mom and dad taught me the value of hard work, and Mom still never misses an opportunity to show off my books to her friends. My wife, Christine, continues to encourage me to keep writing, despite the odd hours; and my daughter, Mia, inspires me with her own passion and zest for life! None of it happens without them.

About the Author

TONY MACCARELLA, or as students past and present call him, "Mr. Mac," has been teaching social studies since 1982, and is currently teaching AP World History and AP Macroeconomics at Saddle River Day School, in Saddle River, NJ.

Prior to this, he taught AP European History at Parsippany Hills High School, in Parsippany, NJ for over 10 years. Additionally, Mr. Mac has taught AP U.S. History, Comparative Governments, Anthropology, Psychology, Microeconomics, and Military History.

Since 2002, Tony has served as a Reader and Table Leader for the AP European History exam for ETS. He is responsible for scoring AP European History exam questions, supervising other readers, and assisting with the clarification of scoring standards. You may also run into Tony at one of the many guest lecturer appearances he makes at social studies conference across the Northeast.

Tony is an avid traveler. He has bicycled across the United States, motorcycled to Sturgis and back, studied in China, and traveled throughout Italy with his wife, family, and students from seven different European History classes.

Also by Tony Maccarella

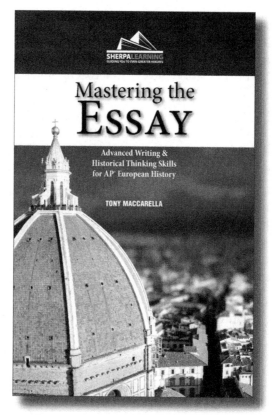

Mastering the Essay

AP* European History Edition

Advanced Writing and Historical Thinking Skills
for AP European History

Instructional Handbook:	isbn 978-0-9905471-3-6
Exercise Workbook:	isbn 978-0-9905471-4-3
Handbook & Workbook Combo:	isbn 978-0-9905471-5-0

www.sherpalearning.com